Golden Key To Success

And Happiness

Verses Kindler Publication

Verses Kindler Publication.

Website: www.verseskindlerpublication.com

Golden Key To Success And Happiness

By: Mr. Sujit Kumar Singh

ISBN: 978-93-49532-81-6

NON-FICTION STORIES 1st Edition

Price: INR 499 / $22

Disclaimer

Golden Key To Success And Happiness is written by Sujit Kumar Singh.

The published work is the original contents of the author and he has done his best to edit and make it plagiarism-free.

The characters may be fictitious or based on real events but they are not meant to hurt anyone's feelings nor portray anything against any caste or system. Any resemblance of names of actual person, place or institute is purely coincidental to carry forward the story.

In case of any plagiarized write-up, the author is solely responsible for it, the publisher would not be responsible for it.

Dedication

This book is dedicated to my parents and the employees of Shreya.

I thank you for your continous motivation and support throughtout my journey.

Index

The Visionary Journey of Sujit Kumar Singh

Sujit Kumar Singh represents a perfect model of determination through his relentless pursuit of goals with a carefully crafted vision along with extraordinary resilience. As a youth from a simple middle-class Indian family in Bihar, Sujit learned to respect work values and ethical behavior. His father, who worked as a schoolteacher, and his mother, who served as a homemaker, passed down their dedication to education and their son. There being no family business to support him, Sujit had to create his path independently, which evolved him from medical school to a pharmaceutical sector tycoon.

The Entrepreneurial Spark

Sujit Kumar Singh chose to study medicine by travelling to Russia following his higher secondary education completion. During his academic period, he learned that he had an entrepreneurial force inside himself. The beginning of his trading enterprise occurred in medical school year two when he sold jackets alongside clothes and pharmaceutical medications. His initial business venture in trading represented the start of his future success in pharmaceutical industry development.

He fully embraced the massive pharmaceutical industry potential when he decided to pursue only pharmaceutical medicines. He took an unconventional step and abandoned his medical studies to pursue a science education because he wanted to develop the necessary foundation for a pharmaceutical business.

The Emergence of Shreya Life Sciences

Sujit Kumar Singh founded Shreya Corporation in Russia in 1993, a venture that specialized in pharmaceutical product distribution. His understanding of the intricacies of international business and his sharp business sense saw the organization grow explosively. The milestone in his career was his acquisition of RALLIS PHARMA from the Tata Group in the year 2000, when he went on to create Shreya Life Sciences.

With his guidance, Shreya Life Sciences prospered to become a market leader in the pharma industry. Not only did the company serve the local market but it also gained a position as a major exporter of pharma products to Russia and other CIS nations. His emphasis on quality and innovation helped Shreya's products gain a solid base in global markets.

Expansion and Diversification

Sujit Kumar Singh's pharmaceutical success was not limited to one field. His entrepreneurial skills and ability to predict the trends of the market enabled him to diversify his business in several fields. He diversified his business into other industries in 2005 by foraying into the entertainment and IT sectors, expanding his business even further. His strategic moves kept on taking place throughout the years, and in 2003, he acquired yet another pharmaceutical company, PLETHICO, enhancing his foothold in the business even more.

2024 was another turning point in his distinguished career when he established a hospitality company, which was one more feather on his cap. His business operations now extended across pharmaceuticals, entertainment, IT, and hospitality, which also depicted his willingness to diversify and succeed in different sectors.

Manufacturing and Employment

Sujit Kumar Singh's contribution is not just distribution-wise. He has two huge manufacturing facilities in India that provide high-quality pharmaceutical drugs and other products as per international standards. These units have been a major contributor to the generation of employment, with Shreya Life Sciences having more than 2,000 employees in India and more than 300 in Russia and the CIS nations.

The substantial professional success achieved by Sujit Kumar Singh has not changed his humble nature and his simple character. The Almighty holds immense power in his eyes, and he follows his religion faithfully. Society is deeply familiar with his charitable works because he conducts numerous benevolent acts that advance social welfare. Sujit Kumar Singh believes in building leadership through respectful and encouraging actions; thus, his most motivational message to staff reads, "WE ARE GREAT BECAUSE YOU ARE GREAT."

A Legacy of Excellence

54-year-old Sujit Kumar Singh is an icon of motivation for future entrepreneurs. From being a medical student to an international business tycoon, his success is the result of unrelenting willpower, long-term strategic thinking, and dedication. With Shreya Life Sciences and all his ventures, he has not only built a successful business empire but also given back considerably to society.

His tale is a powerful reminder that success is not just about monetary progress but about making a lasting difference, driving innovation, and inspiring those around us. Sujit Kumar Singh's journey is not yet complete, and his legacy will certainly go on to inspire future generations.

Chapter 1: Setting the Goals

You find yourself at a crossroad; the road ahead seems to be infinite. Some roads look inviting, some intimidating. In the absence of knowing where you want to be, which road do you take? Now, think of the last time you felt lost-not physically but in your career and personal life. That the time will come when everything done seemed all haphazard and every decision seemed shot in the dark, most people can identify with something.

This feeling is not failure but the lack of a defined objective. It may help to think about it like this: every great achievement in history started as a vision. Whether it was a scientist pushing boundaries, an athlete training for a championship, or a leader transforming an industry, they all had one thing in common: they knew exactly what they were working toward. The same principle applies to you. Without a concrete goal, even the most talented individuals struggle to move forward with purpose.

The first step in establishing an effective goal is to come up with a vision statement. A vision statement is basically a declaration of what you would like to achieve professionally and personally. It expresses your deepest values and long-term aspirations. In this way, the writing of the vision statement sets down your commitment and reminds you constantly of the ultimate destination.

Just as crucial is how your daily activities are aligned to this long-term vision. Every decision you make, no matter how minute, has to bring you closer to your goal. This alignment transforms the abstract dreams into concrete milestones.

Breaking down the large goals into small, actionable benchmarks is a strategy. The vision is great, but daunting and overwhelming until it is divided into manageable steps. Every step represents progress toward the goal and keeps you going.

This doesn't mean you're going straight to success; often, it requires zigzagging in order to deal with the unavoidable challenges and setbacks. Adaptation becomes your ally. Goals will change as the person grows, and refining or widening your vision helps you stay close to your sense of purpose, embracing new chances that come about.

Visualization is another strong tool. If you picture yourself succeeding — imagining that role of leadership, speaking to that conference, or launching that seminal project — your mind becomes imprinted with what it must do to bring it about. Visualization builds confidence and resilience; any goal, no matter how wild, starts to feel within your reach.

Lastly, no purpose stands alone. The power of compelling others to support your cause can then multiply your force. When one's goals relate to those nearby, one achieves a network of like-minded achievers who build individual aspirations toward collective success.

Read this...

The leader specifically recalls the incident when they found out that, after all, setting a proper goal is also important. As a newly graduated pharmaceutical sciences graduate, they were itching to do something meaningful but lacked an actual plan. Slogging through routine paperwork seemed not only mundane but utterly unrelated to any great cause. It wasn't until one sleepless night, staring at the ceiling of their modest apartment, that they stared at that ceiling and asked themselves a life-changing question: What do I really want to do?

It was not a solution that came overnight. But it did require introspection and honesty. They jotted down thoughts in a notebook over the few days, revisiting their childhood dreams and professional aspirations. Slowly, a vision began to take shape: to revolutionize healthcare in underserved regions by becoming a leader in the pharmaceutical industry. That vision became their guiding light.

But having a vision was just the beginning. They spent early in their career fighting reality: putting in long hours, doing the daily grind tasks: writing reports, analyzing data, and assisting with clinical trials. They sometimes get frustrated. "How does this help me change the world?".

One of their mentors gave them a different perspective: "Every great leader started by mastering the basics. If you can't do the small things well, how will you handle the big ones?" This advice shifted their mindset. They began to see every task, however routine, as a building block in their future success. The reports taught them clarity of expression. The clinical trial management taught them precision and teamwork. Each challenge turned into an opportunity for growth.

The biggest blow came when they faced their first major setback: a clinical trial they were supervising turned into a disaster. They suffered significant financial loss, and for themselves, disappointment and frustration ran amok for weeks. Were their dreams too high? Could they even hope to achieve this dream?

Instead of giving up, they decided to treat failure as a lesson. They analyzed the trial in detail, identified where things went wrong, and implemented changes. This experience taught them resilience and reinforced the importance of staying true to their vision, even when the path seemed difficult.
As they gained more experience, their vision changed. They began with a goal of improving healthcare access but came to

realize that systemic change was about influencing policy and driving innovation. This did not dilute the original goal; it enriched it. They embraced the idea that goals should grow with you, adapting to new challenges and opportunities.

Visualization is one of the important aspects in their journey. Often, they visualize themselves speaking to world conferences, spearheading some innovative projects, and inspiring people. This was not just motivation for them; it molded their actions. It instilled in them the confidence to grab opportunities and take calculated risks because they were working toward something bigger than themselves.

Their vision now became a reality over time. They rose through the ranks, led transformative initiatives, and became a respected leader in their field. However, it was not their professional success for which they are most proud; it was the ripple effect of their vision. By sharing their journey, inspiring others, they created a network of individuals who shared a similar mission and amplified their work.

They reflect on that sleepless night in their apartment when they first asked themselves what they truly wanted. That was the night they set a goal, which didn't just change their career, but changed their life.

Actionable Insights

Success, as it can be read in the story of a leader's journey, yields so many valuable things that can instigate readers to take meaningful steps toward their goals. Success is not luck but the product of deliberate action, thoughtful planning, and fixed perseverance. Here are the actionable insights that can help you imbibe these lessons and apply them to your personal and professional life:

Craft a Clear Vision Statement

Knowing exactly where you want to go is the first step to success. A vision statement is not just a lofty idea; it's a roadmap that guides your decisions and actions. Take time to reflect on what you really want to achieve in your career and personal life. Write it down and revisit it regularly. Ask yourself: What legacy do I want to leave behind? How will my actions today contribute to my long-term goals? A clear vision will serve as a constant reminder of your purpose, especially during challenging times.

Align Daily Actions with Long-Term Goals

Setting a goal is just the beginning; the real work lies in ensuring your daily efforts align with that goal. Start each day by identifying tasks that directly contribute to your vision.

Even small steps—a new skill learned, connections made, or one specific area improved at work—are cumulative. It is all about consistency. Indeed, as a leader's story goes, the report they write and the case they manage ultimately contribute to their triumph.

Divide Goals into Workable Milestones

Dreams this big can look so overwhelming and impossible to even consider, especially when broken up into smaller achievable milestones. Instead of becoming an industry leader someday, you try to excel as much as possible in your position. You're developing skills for the next leap, gaining enough experience, or building relationships needed to advance on the career track. Celebrating small wins throughout the process motivates and enhances commitment.

Leverage Failures and Setback

Failure is part of the process, but it also teaches one the greatest. Understanding their failed clinical trial helped the leader transform a loss into a stepping stone for gaining success. When things go awry, take a step back, evaluate what went wrong, and introduce improvements to develop. Learn to treat every challenge as a chance to become better and wiser.

Imagine Your Success

Visualization can be a good tool for solidifying your goals and building up your confidence. Imagine yourself as a leader with a team or launching a new project or affecting your field. This mental training keeps you in line, positive, even when the going gets tough. Remember, if you can see it, you can do it.

Inspire and Engage Others

Goals gain momentum when they resonate beyond yourself. Share your vision with others—mentors, peers, or even your team. Collaboration and shared purpose create a supportive network that amplifies your efforts. Surround yourself with people who believe in your mission and can provide guidance, encouragement, or constructive feedback.

Success is not about the destination. It's about the journey and the person you become in it. Using these actionable insights, you can take control of your life to align with your deepest aspirations.

The leader always says:

"Dream big, act consistently, and never let setbacks define your story. Success begins with a single, clear goal."

Chapter 2: The Power of Self-Discipline

Two people possess similar aptitudes, similar resources, and a parallel opportunity. One of them performs, winning everything he sets his mind to do. The other one cannot succeed, never being able to rise to their full potential. What is the reason behind this? It is not intelligence or luck—it is discipline.

Think back to the last time you set a goal—maybe fit, completing some major work projects, or preparation for an important certification. When you first committed to it, the enthusiasm and motivation were all there, but somewhere along the way, other things started drifting in. There was that sleep button, then social media scrolling, or this illusion that, actually, it was going to take more time than it could. Before you knew it, the deadline loomed, the opportunity slipped away, and you were left with regret.

This is where self-discipline plays the deciding factor between success and stagnation. It is this ability to be committed, not tempted by the short-term and push forward when motivation wavers that makes the dreams achievable. The good news? Discipline isn't a thing you're born with- it's a skill that you can develop. And just like any skill, it requires effort, consistency, and the willingness to move outside your comfort zone.

The story: Gama Pehlwan

Gama Pehlwan was born in 1878 in Amritsar, Punjab, to a wrestling family. As soon as he could walk, he was fascinated by the akharas where men wrestled with one another in the holy sand, their bodies dripping with sweat and determination. Wrestling, though, was not simply a sport in India; it was a way of life, a tradition that passed from generation to generation, and young Gama was determined to be worthy of the legacy he had inherited. But things were not easy for him.

His family fought with poverty, hardly scratching together enough to make ends meet. Survival was a burden, and still, as a child, he did not let it break him. Each morning, before the world woke up, he used to wake up early, wear a cloth on his waist, and go for intense training. His father died when he was a child, and the responsibility of continuing the family legacy was on his frail shoulders. At the age of ten, he participated in a national wrestling competition that took place in Jodhpur. Hundreds of seasoned wrestlers had come, their physiques sculpted after years of unrelenting training.

Among them was Gama, small and modest, but with an intensity in his gaze that was impossible to overlook. The competition involved the wrestlers carrying out a sequence of strength exercises—push-ups, squats, and several other daunting physical challenges. As the rounds went on, several of the tough and experienced wrestlers were eliminated, not being able to sustain the requirements of the test. Yet Gama persisted. He did more than five thousand squats and three thousand push-ups, outdoing even the most renowned pehlwans of his day. His endurance was unparalleled. He didn't survive; he was overwhelmed. The Maharaja of Jodhpur, who attended the match, was so impressed that he officially declared Gama the victor, much to the surprise of his young age. On this day, the world of wrestling took notice. But his actual adventure had just begun. Bravery alone would not do—he had to learn self-control. His training every day was more than the previous one. He used to eat tremendous amounts of milk, almonds, and ghee to power himself. He wrestled with the wrestlers for hours, exerting himself to breaking point. But his most infamous training regimen was something that became a story of grit generations told and retold later.". One day, he brought a newborn calf home. It was tiny and delicate, hardly strong enough to stand on its own legs.

Gama lifted it up and put it on his shoulders, feeling the warm softness of its body.

It was an unusual exercise, but he knew what he was doing. Every morning, religiously, he would lift the calf and walk around with it. The villagers thought it was funny at first, seeing a young wrestler carrying a small animal on his back as training. They laughed unaware of the deep wisdom in what he did. Months turned into weeks, and the calf increased in size. As its legs developed and its body gained shape, Gama still carried it, his muscles becoming stronger each day. The initial ease of carrying the calf soon became a test. It weighed almost 150 kilograms when it was one year old, and yet he still carried it with ease.

His physiology adjusted to the added weight, and what was once a routine training exercise became a demonstration of his patience and discipline. The years went by, and the calf matured into a giant buffalo, now tipping the scale at more than 500 kilograms. By that time, Gama was one of the most respected and feared wrestlers in India. His physique was chiseled out of pure hard work, his muscles iron-like, and his stamina unmatchable. Buffalo-lifting had turned him into a force of nature. But in addition to physical power, it had instilled in him the spirit of discipline—the belief that real power isn't forged overnight but hammered out through unyielding persistence.

Increasingly, his reputation drew him against some of the strongest wrestlers in India, and he emerged undefeated. His technique, quickness, and sheer determination made him unbeatable. Yet he was not satisfied to be a champion within his own nation. He aimed for the world. In 1910, he went to England to challenge the top wrestlers of the world. Initially, the British organizers were not willing to allow an Indian to compete, underrating him due to his shorter height.

But when he challenged and beat some of their strongest men, they had no option but to accept his skill. One of his most legendary battles was against Polish world champion Stanislaus Zbyszko. The two wrestlers battled each other for over two hours with neither giving quarter. Gama's power and stamina were never matched, but the European forms of wrestling were unfamiliar to him. In spite of the torrid battle, the bout resulted in a tie. But in the rematch, Gama beat Zbyszko within a minute, and he became the world champion. Back in India, he was hailed as a national hero. His wins weren't his alone; they were a reflection of India's power, a testament to what discipline and hard work could do.

But even after achieving the height of success, he never forgot his humble beginnings. He continued his hard training, waking up at the break of day as always, challenging himself to the limits as always, and following the maxims that had created him. As the years went by, his legend only grew stronger. Accounts of his training, his strength, and his unshakeable devotion to discipline inspired generations to come. The story of the calf he had lifted as a child became an allegory of perseverance and patience, reminding people that success doesn't happen overnight but is forged, bit by bit, by daily efforts. Even in retirement, he was a force to be reckoned with, teaching those who came after him, young wrestlers, as much about being great not simply physically, but mentally. For Gama, strength wasn't simply muscle mass; it was mentality. It was having the will to carry on, the ability to stick with it and to be unyielding in commitment even in secret. His influence went far beyond wrestling. Even at the time of the partition of India in 1947, he utilized his power to save innumerable individuals from communal violence, and he became a symbol of courage and unity. Even with his huge physical strength, he never utilized it for anything else but for his principles. He was not merely a wrestler; he was a man of character, discipline, and unshakable determination. And as he aged, his body, once strong enough to lift a mature buffalo, slowly lost strength.

But never did his spirit. To his dying days, he was an example of what human determination could accomplish. When he died in 1960, the world lost not only a great wrestler but an icon of discipline, a legend who had demonstrated through his life that greatness is not talent or luck but hard work, done every day, until success is no longer an option but a certainty. Gama Pehlwan's tale is one that is even today narrated, not merely in India but globally, because it serves to remind us of the fact that discipline is a bridge between desired outcomes and fruition. Whether with a calf lift or against the world champions, his life remained a testament that real strength involves dedication, waiting, and sheer will to keep going.

Actionable Insights: Building Unshakable Discipline

Start Small, Stay Consistent

Discipline isn't built overnight. It begins with small, intentional actions repeated consistently. If waking up at 4:30 AM seems too extreme, start with a more manageable change, like waking up 30 minutes earlier. The key is consistency—doing it every day until it becomes second nature.

Eliminate Decision Fatigue

Every day we make hundreds of small decisions regarding what to wear, what to eat, or when to hit the gym. All these add up to diminish our willpower over time. To stay disciplined, automate all the decisions. Plan your clothing for the day the night before, decide on a fixed meal chart, and dedicate specific hours of the day only to work. The lesser one depends on the motivation, the easier it gets to be in control.

Practice the Power of Time-Blocking

Possibly one of the best ways to create discipline is through time-blocking. Instead of trying to fit in the important things, schedule them. Assign a specific time for exercise, deep work, and personal development. Treat these time blocks like any other commitment, one that cannot be rescheduled like a meeting with the CEO.

Leverage Accountability

Without anybody to answer to, self-discipline can lead to many problems. Joining a study group, finding an accountability partner, or making a public commitment to your objectives are all ways to establish external accountability. You have a far higher possibility of following through when someone else is looking.

Establish a Morning Schedule

You will spend the remainder of your day in the same manner as you began it. Create a productive morning ritual rather than grabbing your phone first thing in the morning. Establish a routine that prepares you for success, whether it be reading, writing in a journal, exercising, or meditation.

Learn to Say No

A disciplined person knows that agreeing to every request is a surefire path to failure. Learn to say no to distractions, unnecessary meetings, and commitments that don't serve your purpose. Your time and energy are limited—be jealous of them.

Change Your Perception of Obstacles as Chances

Most people are in a pattern to avoid discomfort, but disciplined people are comfortable with it. Instead of saying, "This is too hard," turn around and say, "This will help me grow." That's how one master challenges into becoming rewarding rather than exhausting.

Track Your Progress

What gets measured gets managed. Track your disciplined habits; it could be writing every day, exercising at a consistent level, or lowering screen time. Use a habit tracker or journal to celebrate small wins and motivate yourself.

Reward Yourself Strategically

Discipline isn't about deprivation; it's about balance. Reward yourself for consistency. If you complete a week of early morning workouts, treat yourself to a movie night. The key is to ensure rewards don't undo progress—choose reinforcements that align with your goals.

Cultivate Grit and Resilience

There will be those days when all you want is to give up. On that day, ask yourself why you started. Remember the inspiring stories of disciplined persons, listen to motivational talks, and envision what you will enjoy in the future. It's what separates an extraordinary person from an average person: the push to continue working even when he or she feels like giving up.

Whatever the mind can conceive and believe,it can achieve.

Chapter 3: Developing a Growth Mindset

Have you ever caught yourself saying, "I'm just not good at this" or "Some people are born talented, and I'm not one of them"? If so, you're not alone. Most of us, at some point, have believed that our abilities are set in stone—that intelligence, creativity, and skills are things you either have or don't. But what if that belief was the very thing holding you back?

Imagine two people struggling with the same problem. One person struggles and immediately concludes they are not cut out for it. They give up, assuming that failure proves their limitations. The other, equally challenged, views the struggle differently. Instead of seeing failure as a dead-end, they see it as feedback—a signal that they need to adjust, learn, and keep going. Over time, this second person improves, adapts, and eventually masters the skill. What separates them? Not intelligence. Not talent. But mindset.

This difference in thinking has been deeply studied by psychologists, most notably Carol Dweck, who coined the terms fixed mindset and growth mindset. A fixed mindset is the belief that our abilities are innate and unchangeable—either you're good at something or you're not. A growth mindset, on the other hand, is the belief that abilities can be developed through effort, learning, and perseverance. People with a growth mindset see failure not as a sign of inadequacy, but as an opportunity to improve.

Take any high achiever—athletes, business leaders, artists, or innovators—and you'll find that their success wasn't just a result of raw talent. It was their willingness to work, fail, adapt, and try again. Michael Jordan was cut from his high school basketball team before becoming one of the greatest players of all time. Oprah Winfrey was told she wasn't fit for television. Thomas Edison failed thousands of times before inventing the lightbulb. The reason they succeeded wasn't because they were born exceptional—it was because they believed they could grow.

But that isn't the psyche of only the world's super achievers. It applies to anyone toiling toward some form of betterment: becoming a high performer at work, learning a new skill, or more personal goals. The way you think about yourself determines the way you behave. If you think you are bad at something and will always be lousy, you won't bother making an effort to change. But if you think you can or you think you can't, you are right.

Coming into a growth mindset requires your approach to be different. Challenges, failure and even feedback. No longer should you run when the going is tough. It should be less likely that mistakes frighten you and instead teach you. Moreover, instead of saying, "I can't do this", you say this one little word: yet.

The Bamboo Farmer: A Lesson in Growth Mindset

He lived in a quiet village, nestled between rolling green hills and misty mountains. The man's name was Lao Wei. He was a Chinese farmer. Wisdom and patience, characteristics passed down from generations of farmers, were identified with his nature. Yet nothing tested either his patience or his belief in growth more than the day he decided to plant bamboo.

Lao Wei has always been infatuated with the bamboo groves towering everywhere across certain stretches of China. He was interested in their pliability, which allows them to resist the sturdiest gusts, and in the ability of some to stand unmoved against stormy gusts. On the first morning of spring, struck by such an impression, he resolved to develop his own plantations of the same bamboo, a place outside his home full of fertile lands where he finally planted the seed.

Every morning, before the sun had fully risen, Lao Wei would step outside with a wooden bucket full of water. He poured it gently over the soil, ensuring that the seed was nourished. He tended to it with the same care he gave his other crops, checking for any signs of life. A week passed. Then a month. Then six months. The soil remained undisturbed, silent, refusing to reveal what lay beneath.

Other farmers in the village began to take notice of Lao Wei's persistence. Some admired his dedication, while others found it amusing.

"You're wasting your time, old friend," said Zhang, a fellow farmer. "Why not plant something that will actually grow? Look at my rice fields. In just a few months, I'll have a full harvest."

Lao Wei just smiled. "Growth takes time, Zhang. Some things require deeper roots before they can rise.

As the months turned into a full year, doubt began to creep into Lao Wei's mind. Was he watering an empty dream? Had he planted a bad seed? He had expected some progress, a tiny green sprout, anything to prove that his efforts were not in vain. But despite his worries, he made a choice: he would continue.

Another year went by. Yet, nothing seemed to come out of his hard work. The villagers were no longer laughing; they started to pity him.

"Lao Wei, don't be stubborn," said an elderly woman from the market. "Nature is telling you that this bamboo will not grow. Let it go."

But Lao Wei learned something valuable in the process. He realized that growth is not always visible. The most important changes happen beneath the surface, in the places we cannot see. He did not let failure define him. Instead, he adjusted his mindset. If he was to succeed, he had to believe that progress was happening, even if he could not witness it directly.

He continued. Every day, he continued to water the place where his seed had been buried. He dug around the soil to get more sunlight into it. He talked to the seed, telling it stories of the tall bamboo forests it will one day join. Though he saw nothing that could excite him, he did not lose faith.

By the third year, Lao Wei had grown so accustomed to his routine that it no longer felt like a struggle. His hands worked the soil without any hesitation, and his mind found peace in the rhythm of nurturing. He stopped worrying about the end result and started embracing the process itself.

Some of the villagers merely turned their heads in passing and whispered something about his "stupid devotion." Others had moved on to other things and did not pay any more attention to the man. The only ones who still attended to his daily ritual were the children, who found it quite fascinating.

"Why are you watering the ground if nothing is growing, Uncle Wei?" a curious boy asked.

Lao Wei crouched down and smiled. "Because it is growing, little one. You just can't see it yet. Everything strong in life begins with deep roots."

Deep inside, he knew that even though he could not see the bamboo, something was happening below the surface. It was strengthening its foundation, anchoring itself into the earth, preparing for the moment it would finally emerge.

Then, in the fifth year, something miraculous happened.

One morning, just as the sun kissed the horizon, Lao Wei noticed a small green shoot breaking through the soil. It was barely visible, but it was there. His heart leapt with joy. After all this time, after years of silent effort, the bamboo had finally decided to rise.

But the real miracle was yet to come.

In the next weeks, that little shoot started growing at a rate that could be considered astounding. What would have taken five years to prepare now unfolded within weeks. Bamboo shot up from the ground: it reached 90 feet within six weeks. The villagers, who had been mocking Lao Wei, were now standing and staring with mouths agape, unable to believe their eyes.

"How can this be?" Zhang asked, shaking his head. "One moment, nothing existed; now—this!"

Lao Wei smiled knowingly. "The bamboo has been growing all along. It was just working under the covers, building its roots that would enable it to grow so fast at the right time."

The Growth Mindset: Learning from the Bamboo

The story of Lao Wei's bamboo plantation is more than just a tale of patience. It is a lesson in the growth mindset—the belief that progress is always happening, even when we can't see it.

Most people give up on their dreams because they always want to achieve them overnight. They start up a new business and, because it does not turn a profit immediately, conclude that they failed. They embark on learning a new skill, but when it doesn't go right, they give up on it. They set goals, but when it doesn't start happening overnight, they give up.

But like the bamboo, real growth is often hidden beneath the surface. The long, unseen effort is what builds the foundation for later success. If Lao Wei had given up in the first year, he would have never seen the towering bamboo forest he had always dreamed of. His belief, his persistence, and his ability to trust the process were what made the difference.

This is the crux of a growth mindset. Instead of taking challenges as proof of our limitations, we must take them as opportunities to develop resilience. Instead of dreading failure, we must acknowledge it as part of the journey. And instead of giving up when progress seems invisible, we must trust that every effort, no matter how small, is contributing to something greater.

Years later, when Lao Wei stood beneath the tall bamboo he nurtured, he thought back on those long years of uncertainty. For him, the biggest growth had not been in the bamboo itself but within him-thus stronger, more patient, and more determined.

And so, he held his story for any ear: to entice them to keep going on their own journeys. "Do not be discouraged if success does not come quickly," he would say. "You are like the bamboo—growing deep roots, preparing for your moment to rise.

Life is, like farming, most rewarding for the ones with patience in nourishing their dreams, with courage enough to persevere even in periods of time where the advancement was invisible to them, and the wisdom of realizing that, always and only always, there was growth under it all.

Actionable Insights from the Bamboo Farmer's Story

The story of the Chinese farmer's bamboo plantation holds powerful lessons about patience, persistence, and the importance of a growth mindset. While the farmer saw no visible progress for years, his unwavering belief in the process led to astonishing results. This mirrors the journey of personal and professional growth—progress isn't always immediate, but with consistency and resilience, success is inevitable. Here are key actionable insights from the story and how you can apply them to your own life and career.

1. Long-term thinking is a powerful thing

Many people expect speedy results. They lose interest and quit when they do not get immediate results. An experience learned from the bamboo farmer is that real success often involves a long, unseen period of growth. Because what happens is invisible doesn't mean it's not happening. Anything you do as practice—whether learning, building, or career advancement—is like watering your seed. Believe in the process, and stay patient.

Action Steps:

- Set long-term goals and then break them down into small, manageable stages.
- Keep track of progress in a journal, even when it feels slow.
- Remind yourself that growth is happening, even if you can't see it yet.

2. Cultivate Patience and Persistence

Had he not kept trying in the second or third year, the farmer would never have witnessed what amazing growth his bamboo plant could experience. More importantly, in life, many people quit just when they are at the point where they are going to experience a breakthrough. The reason for great things to happen is consistent effort over time regardless of the setbacks that may occur.

Action Steps:

- Identify a skill or goal that requires long-term effort and commit to it.

- Develop daily habits that support your growth, no matter how small.

- When the going gets tough, remind yourself that persistence pays off.

3. Build a Strong Foundation Before Expecting Results

Before the bamboo grew 90 feet, it required deep, firm roots underground. This is very important for the person working his way to succeed. The period of learning or self-improvement may sometimes seem unfruitful, but it is just the foundation from which future breakthroughs shall be made. Whether you train for a marathon, learn to speak a new language, or grow a new business, that effort you expend now will back your future efforts.

Action Steps:

- Spend time learning and developing basic skills.
- Build a solid base of knowledge and expertise before expecting rapid success.
- Consistency in effort, even if progress is not immediately visible, is key.

4. Train Your Subconscious Mind for Success

The farmer didn't just plant the seed and forget about it; he watered it every day. We must feed our minds with good thoughts, self-belief, and constructive habits every day. Many people fail because they allow doubt, negativity, and fear to take control. A growth mindset means that you are always reinforcing positive beliefs about yourself and your potential.

Action Steps

- Practice affirmations that reinforce your belief in growth and improvement.

Surround yourself with supportive people who encourage your progress.

- Read books and listen to podcasts that promote a growth mindset.

5. See Failure as a Part of Growth

Many people throw in the towel when they face failure, thinking that it indicates they are not capable. However, failure is just feedback-it is part of the learning curve. The farmer could have concluded after a year that the seed would never grow, but he continued to cultivate it. In life, setbacks should be taken as learning opportunities and not as roadblocks.

Action Steps:

- Failure should be reframed as an opportunity for learning and improvement.

- When faced with a setback, ask yourself, "What can I learn from this?"

- Keep moving forward, knowing that persistence leads to eventual success.

6. Stay Consistent Even When Motivation Fades

There is no visible sign in the early years that your efforts are working, yet the farmer continues. Motivation will get you started, but it is a discipline that keeps you going. The habit of showing up every day even when you do not feel like it is what keeps you on the path to long-term success.

Action Steps:

- Create a schedule or routine that keeps you accountable.

- Find a mentor or accountability partner to encourage consistency.

- Focus on the process rather than the outcome, incremental improvements each day add up.

7. Trust the Process and Stay Committed

The farmer never doubted that the seed would grow eventually; he just kept working. Doubt and impatience quite often derail anyone from his goals. A growth mindset requires trust in the process, faith in your abilities, and commitment to continue, no matter how long it takes.

Action Steps:

- Remind yourself that success comes with time and effort.
- Look at what is within your power to control - your actions, mindset, and persistence.
- Small wins help one stay motivated to continue moving.

8. Translate These Principles Into Everyday Life

These lessons from the story of the bamboo farmer can be applied in any area of life, whether advancing in your career, improving personal relationships, or developing a new skill. Growth takes time, and every small action contributes to the bigger picture.

Action Steps:

- Choose one goal to apply these lessons to immediately.
- Commit to daily improvement and track your progress.
- Remember that every great success story begins with an unseen effort.

The patience, persistence, and faith of a bamboo farmer in unseen growth well illustrates anyone's pursuit of achievement. Don't give up on your dreams; have faith in this process; one day, you will note the fruits of such efforts in ways you could never have imagined.

You are the master of your destiny; you are the captain of your soul.

Chapter 4. Time Management: The Ultimate Asset

Time is the most egalitarian but merciless resource. Each person, a billionaire CEO or a university student alike, has an equal twenty-four hours a day. Success or mediocrity is determined by how one spends these hours. In contrast to money, which can be made, saved, and invested, time is spent only once. Once time is gone, it will never return. This makes time the most precious asset, one that requires deliberate planning and intentional use.

The greatest obstacle individuals have with time is not insufficient time but rather an inability to prioritize. Everyday life presents numerous distractions—important emails, constant meetings, and eleventh-hour requests—all of which compel people to respond rather than plan. A structure keeps activities productive thus helping us avoid being too busy without real accomplishment. The Eisenhower Matrix alongside other prioritization models aid time management by identifying urgent activities from significant ones which enable people to invest their time in important endeavors. The Pareto Principle demonstrates a relationship between 80% of results coming from 20% of efforts so businesses need to recognize the key tasks that deliver maximum outcomes.

Time management exists to find equilibrium instead of creating efficiency alone. Workers often give higher importance to urgent short-term responsibilities over future objectives thus leading them to experience burnout and fail to seize valuable opportunities. Long-term success depends on time management expertise through learning when to reject responsibilities together with proper work assignments and clear target selection.

Exceptional time managers use strategic decisions in critical instances to achieve deadline success while developing an aligned strategic vision. One of the greatest historical instances of managing time well combined with making sound choices and prioritization features in the story of King Harishchandra whose truthfulness became legendary enough to face an epic timeline obstacle.

Have you heard about Harishchandra?

The worldwide community admired Harishchandra for his fairness and honesty which made him known as a renowned king. People from his domain prospered under his leadership and deeply respected him. But no trial of integrity is without cost, and his highest test started when the wise man Vishwamitra resolved to test his commitment to truth. One day, Vishwamitra came before Harishchandra and declared that in a dream, the king had pledged to give his whole kingdom in charity. Harishchandra, a keeper of promises, did not plead. At once, he yielded his throne, his wealth, and his dominions. Strip of his royality, he departed his palace with his wife, Taramati, and his young son, Rohitashva, with only the clothes on their backs.

But Vishwamitra was not pleased. He asked for a donation as a settlement of the pledge once and for all. Harishchandra, having no wealth now, had to do something to raise money to honor his pledge. Time was running out. He had to do it in haste, for any delay would involve going back on his word. Without hesitation, he set out for Kashi (Varanasi), hoping to get employment that would enable him to earn enough to honor the sage's request.

With few choices, Harishchandra did the unthinkable—he became a laborer at a cremation ground, a job deemed unclean for a man of his standing. His work was straightforward but emotionally draining: he had to charge fees from bereaved families before cremation rites could be performed. In spite of his own misery, he stuck to his duty, weighing the short-term necessity of survival against his ultimate goal of remaining faithful to his principles.

Time went on relentlessly, and Harishchandra suffered years of adversity. But just when he believed the worst was over, fate struck him another harsh blow. His son, Rohitashva, took a serious illness and passed away.

Taramati, now shattered by sorrow, brought their child's corpse to the same cremation grounds where Harishchandra was employed. But with a cruel irony of fate, she failed to recognize her husband in his pitiful condition. According to tradition, she sought the caretaker's permission and requested that she be allowed to cremate her son. Harishchandra, although heartbroken, was duty-bound. He had to charge her for the cremation, just like he did to all other mourning families.

Taramati begged, saying she had nothing left—no jewellery, no house, and no riches. All she had was grief and loss. The time was agonizing. Time was running out, and Harishchandra was faced with an impossible choice. Should he keep his word and ask his wife for payment? Or should he bend the rules for his own sorrow, transgressing the very rules he had lived by? The choice needed to be made immediately—there was no time to think.

In that instant of need, divine justice descended. The gods, touched by his unshakeable commitment to truth and time-based integrity, brought his son back to life and restored his kingdom. Harishchandra's capacity to give top priority to his responsibility, make choices in extreme pressure, and reconcile immediate needs with long-term principles had resulted in his final redemption.

Actionable Insights

Harishchandra's tale is not merely one of truthfulness—it's a lesson in the management of time. Each choice he made was governed by a keen sense of the constraints of time, reminding us of three key lessons:

- The first is urgent prioritization. Harishchandra was constantly being tested, each test forcing him to make an instant decision between temporary comfort and permanent uprightness. Rather than frittering away time on loss, he only thought about what to do next. In life, experts too experience such moments—urgency, setbacks, and clashing responsibilities. Time management lies in being able to prioritize what's important and allocate time for it. The Eisenhower Matrix can assist in such situations by separating urgent and important tasks.

- The second lesson is to balance short-term needs and long-term goals. Harishchandra's labour at the cremation ground was a step towards a purpose—he was well aware that temporary suffering would take him to his destination. It is simple in today's quick-paced world to get overwhelmed with immediate tasks, emails, and meetings and not have time to think strategically. Effective leaders make time for long-term planning and ensure that every day's efforts are aligned towards larger goals. The Pareto Principle states that 80% of outcomes result from 20% of effort. By prioritizing high-impact activities over spreading oneself too thin, one can maximize finite time.

- Lastly, the third lesson is making consequential decisions within a time-sensitive situation. Harish Chandra had seconds to make a decision about whether to honour his responsibility or bend the rules for selfish reasons. Each professional encounters such high-stakes choices, whether in business deals, project timelines, or crisis intervention. The skill of remaining calm, thinking through possibilities at lightning speed, and making bold decisions sets great leaders apart from others. Great time managers count on preparation and simplicity—being aware of their priorities ahead of time so when high-stakes decisions surface, they have the ability to move rapidly without hesitation.

In today's world, CEOs, entrepreneurs, and working professionals all have time pressures that require accuracy and strategic thought. A CEO working on a high-impact project needs to weigh client expectations against the well-being of employees alongside deadlines.

An investor needs to decide which startups to invest in based on future market potential and not short-term trends. A student needs to weigh instant academic demands against long-term professional progress. In all these situations, time is the determining factor that governs success or failure.

Finally, time is not something to be controlled—it is something to be conquered. Anyone who grasps this reality, such as Harishchandra, makes timely decisions that shape their fate.

The way to get started is to quit talking and begin doing.

Chapter 5. The Art of Communication:

Influence Through Words

Communication exists beyond affirmative word sequences since it establishes the basis for influence; leadership development, and overall achievement. A clear, confident and empathetic delivery of thoughts turns ordinary messages into transformative forces that create change. The capacity to communicate proves essential regardless of addressing an executive board cultivating student engagement or maintaining widespread viewer connection.

Throughout the past, leaders used their words to establish dominant ideas while encouraging people to take direction which created enduring consequences. The art of communication serves as an essential skill which enables nations to follow their political leaders and entrepreneurs to present revolutionary concepts. Messages become easy to understand through clarity and credibility grows from confidence while deep connections develop because of empathy. A master communicator listens first and then adapts their approach through engagement to speak effectively.

Read about Oprah Winfrey

Oprah Winfrey stands as a critical example of someone who masters effective communication. Through her journey from poverty towards becoming a worldwide media powerhouse Oprah turned stories into emotional connections with her audience. Her authentic attachment to others and exceptional interpersonal abilities made her a prominent influential speaker. Her philosophy centred on using communication for inspiring change through interviews and speeches along with her philanthropic activities.

Effective communication methods which media moguls use cannot be reserved for their profession only. A company's future rests on how well its CEO presents to doubtful investors thus demonstrating these competencies also work fundamentally in business. A clear vision backed by persuasion combined with message adaptation for various audiences and steady handling of concerns produces both professional success and failure. The communication elements functioned differently in both Oprah Winfrey's path to influence and a CEO's investor presentation.

Oprah Winfrey exceeded numerous obstacles to enter the media. During her birth year of 1954, Oprah entered the world into poor circumstances which eventually led to experiencing both physical mistreatment and domestic turmoil. Words were the single point which never changed since she developed this passion when she was young. Her grandmother raised Oprah and the power of storytelling became evident to her through her church recitations and her books. At the beginning of her life, Oprah discovered that words served as instruments to achieve dominance and emotional impact and obtain entry to different possibilities.

At nineteen years old she made her first appearance in television news broadcasting in Nashville. The moment marked an important achievement because few Black women existed as media representatives during that period. Her intelligence and presence posed difficulties for her when she tried to deliver news through the technical inflexible anchor tone. She discovered her true broadcaster voice through the host role on "People Are Talking" at Baltimore. Through her human connection style she transformed her talk show into a hit because she treated the audience as empathetic human beings rather than mere subjects. Oprah used listening as her primary way to interact with people rather than asking questions. The strong relationship she developed with her viewers became permanent because of her listening habits.

The 1986 launch of "The Oprah Winfrey Show' brought unprecedented transformations to daytime television. Oprah created an environment based on trust that differentiated her talk show from others focused on sensationalism. She maintained equal respect and interest when speaking to both the Hollywood elite and ordinary members of the population. She handled hard subjects regarding race, gender, and trauma by showing both courage and sympathy towards her viewers. Her way of speaking served to understand rather than control others.

Oprah created her most memorable impact through her interview with Nelson Mandela after he finished his prison term. In the interview with Nelson Mandela, Oprah portrayed his triumphs to demonstrate his strength which connected to viewers around the world. Oprah delivered her message about authentic communication when she addressed Stanford University students in 2004. She declared that the most important life lesson she received amounts to personal responsibility for everything that happens to you. Sitting around waiting for anyone to fix help or rescue you results in a destructive waste of time. I felt her message deeply because she genuinely presented her message.

The foundation of Oprah's achievement derived from her masterful combination of clarity with confident and feeling-empathetic ways. Her objective in speaking surpassed mere vocalization because she used words to transform situations.

Corporate businesses essentially require the same communication principles for obtaining investments throughout their processes. A tech startup CEO prepares to deliver the most important business presentation because it will determine the outcome of their career. Investors exhibited doubt about the innovative AI-driven platform that their company had developed. A powerful pitch strategy was required by the company to create confidence from doubt before achieving their largest funding round to date.

When the CEO approached the stage they understood factual information would not stand alone as a sufficient strategy. The investors required more than statistical data since they needed to see a clear strategic vision. The company executives desired people to trust their future trajectory. The CEO described a future scenario where businesses could translate their data into decisions easily while AI stood as their reliable advisory system. The audience leaned in. The application of jargon-free communication enabled the CEO to convert complicated information into easy-to-understand examples.

Next came confidence. When presenting to the audience the CEO maintained a steady tone while giving essential points without providing excessive information. Both their tone and body signals gave off a reliable and confident impression. To prevent future problems they analyzed possible concerns so they could resolve them clearly in advance. The executive team directly addressed demanding questions regarding competition and scalability by admitting challenges and then delivering solutions to surmount them.

Empathy was the decisive factor that made investors choose the presenting company. The CEO designed the investor pitch to focus on how the company benefited shareholders instead of only highlighting business success. "We understand your concerns. Your search targets a sustainable enterprise along with innovative capabilities. Our strategy includes long-term plans which generate growth opportunities for stakeholders across the board."

After the presentation concluded the investors displayed great enthusiasm and proved ready to support the enterprise in its path forward. The start-up conducted funding rounds beyond what analysts estimated which demonstrated that effective communication involves establishing connections rather than promoting things.

Communication arts function as a learnable skill which any person can acquire. We can use these three practical ideas whenever we need to communicate effectively in daily situations.

Actionable Insights

- First, clarity is key. Every communication needs to be direct and organized no matter how many people are hearing it from individuals to vast audiences. Any technical language should be avoided when possible while maintaining straightforward communication at all times. A direct message carries maximum impact when communicated. Identify the main point you desire your audience members to retain before delivering your speech.

- Second, confidence is contagious. The message of people stand behind individuals who demonstrate self-assurance. The message becomes clear through self-assurance rather than arrogance. Keep your posture strong while meeting people's gaze while speaking in a stable voice quality. Applications serve as the most effective solution to manage nervousness when speaking. Preparation leads to the natural delivery of your message.

- Finally, empathy builds trust. Great speaking ability does not guarantee successful communication because the best communicators remain excellent listeners. Projection of understanding to the audience should be coupled with attention to their worries followed by appropriate message adjustment. Every business interaction and everyday dialogue becomes stronger when you demonstrate an authentic interest in understanding the perspectives of others.

If you acquire good communication abilities then you will unlock new professional opportunities besides being able to initiate transformative change. People who lead companies conduct talk shows and deliver speeches use identical principles to bring success to their actions.

According to Oprah Winfrey's entire career exhibition words possess the energy to remodel human existence. During his presentation, the CEO exemplified how turning doubt into self-assurance is possible.

Advancing communication skills requires more than speaking abilities because they allow you to infuse influence and inspiration and create meaningful effects in the world.

You are the master of your destiny; you are the captain of your soul.

Chapter 6. Winning with Relationships

Achieving success happens only through teamwork. Every achievement depends on the presence of other people whom a person encounters while reaching their goals even if they demonstrate talent or work hard or show creativity. Relationships formed at the start of human civilization stand as the fundamental foundation for reaching success in all its forms: business achievements as well as leadership roles and personal fulfilment. Achieving the skill to create bonds, earn trust and maintain positive relationships stands among the most valuable abilities a person can obtain.

Creating strong personal bonds goes beyond maintaining professional networking connections and cultivating favorable connections. The processes involve building trust alongside presenting authentic behavior while delivering meaningful value to someone else's life. People easily detect transactions in human relationships versus authentic connections. People whose relationships grow from sincere honesty and genuine respect create lasting meaningful bonds. Sharing a meaningful conversation with someone can develop into a friendship that lasts forever. Similarly, sharing an experience or allowing insight into yourself transforms mere acquaintances into eternal friends.

People face the main difficulty because they adopt distinct ways to handle their relationships. A portion of humanity exhibits natural exuberance to thrive socially but there exists another group of individuals who gravitate toward intimate one-on-one interactions. Personality matters less than skills in trust building networking and opportunity detection when it comes to making winning relationships.

History remembers the extraordinary bond of friendship in ancient India between Krishna and Sudama which set their destinies in motion. An authentic relationship created through trust and kindness transformed lives beyond all expectations in the story of these friends.

Sudama and Krishna

Sudama and Krishna were childhood friends who grew up together as close companions in the same gurukul, with the same guru. As Krishna was a prince, charming and intelligent, Sudama came from a poor family. Their relationship endured despite this contrast due to mutual respect, jokes, and experiences in studying together.

Over time, their fates were completely different. Krishna emerged as a great ruler of Dwarka, governing a kingdom full of wealth, intelligence, and power. Sudama had a life of hardship. He dwelled in a poor hut with his wife and kids, just able to meet ends. Despite this, however, Sudama never asked anyone for anything.

But then one day, when his children were crying from hunger, Sudama's wife pressed him to go to Krishna for help. He was hesitant at first, not wanting to turn a childhood friendship into begging. But ultimately, he yielded—not for himself, but out of concern for his family. His wife made a small package of poha (flattened rice) as a present for Krishna, the only thing they could offer.

As Sudama drew near to Dwarka's great gates, he was in his place no more. The golden chariots, the nobles who were clad to perfection, the great palaces—these were things from which he did not belong. Yet Krishna would not forget an old friend. The instant Krishna espied Sudama, he hurried towards him with open arms. He took Sudama into the palace, washed his feet as a sign of respect, and honored him as a royal guest.

They talked for hours, reminiscing about their boyhood, sharing a chuckle over old stories, and indulging in the love they always shared. Krishna, observing the little package Sudama had under his arm, eagerly inquired what he had brought along. Blushing, Sudama hung back, but Krishna, never one to reserve himself, pulled out the little package and enjoyed the simple poha with zest. For him, this wasn't food—

this was love, the one thing most valuable to him that he could obtain.

Sudama never once spoke of his troubles. He could not find the heart to ask Krishna for assistance, as he was overcome by the affection and regard Krishna had extended to him. Having stayed overnight in the palace, he departed early the following morning, happy for the hospitality of their friendship but assuming that he had come back empty-handed.

When Sudama arrived home, though, he was in for a surprise. Instead of his simple hut stood a beautiful house, full of food, wealth, and comfort. Krishna had secretly made sure that Sudama and his family never went without again, all without his friend ever having to request it.

This tale beautifully describes the strength of relationships. Sudama never approached Krishna with selfishness, nor did Krishna assist Sudama based on sympathy. Their relationship was founded on mutual trust, respect, and actual connection, and it goes to show that the strongest relationships are those where both parties appreciate one another for what they are and not for what they can provide.

Actionable Insights

Sudama and Krishna's tale points to the essence of succeeding with relationships: genuineness, trust, and seeing the worth of genuine connections. These essentials work in both professional and personal arenas, defining careers, companies, and individual achievement.

- The first and most important lesson is establishing trust with authenticity. Human beings are instinctively attracted to genuine people. Krishna did not differentiate in the treatment of Sudama simply because he was poor; he appreciated their friendship more than money. Likewise, successful business and life partnerships flourish when individuals demonstrate real interest, honesty, and dependability. Whether a CEO builds trust with staff or an entrepreneur develops a brand, long-term achievement results from authenticity rather than strategy.

- The second lesson is networking in a manner that feels natural to you. Not all are outgoing social butterflies, and that is fine. Some function better in crowds, and some need meaningful, one-on-one connections. Networking isn't about business card collection—it's about meaningful connections. Introverts can build strong connections through an emphasis on substance-rich, in-depth discussions, follow-up notes with genuine comments, and contributing value in insight or encouragement. Extroverts can leverage their energy by attending events, introducing people to each other, and maintaining a strong presence in professional circles. The key is to network in a way that feels natural rather than forced.

- Lastly, the third lesson is seeing and fostering opportunities for relationships. At times, the most significant relationships are initiated by an informal conversation. A friendly cup of coffee with a mentor might become a long-term alliance. CEOs attribute success to one meeting that altered their professional course. Seeing potential in relationships, spending time to cultivate them, and being receptive to new relationships can result in unexpected success.

A real-life instance is from a CEO who had once sat down with a top executive at a conference. What began as a casual conversation over coffee led to a string of follow-ups, joint efforts, and finally, a big business alliance that redefined the future of both their organizations. Just like Sudama's meeting with Krishna, the first encounter did not come with any expectation, but the genuineness of their connection gave rise to incredible results.

Wining with relationships is not a matter of strategy—it's about making the effort, trusting others, and being able to look past the surface level. The greatest achievers in the world recognize that the biggest asset they have isn't their abilities or their money—it's the relationships they build.

The most common cause of failure is the habit of quitting when one is overtaken by temporary defeat.

Chapter 7. The Power of Empathy in Leadership

Leadership maintains its core value in serving people even though it is commonly connected to power and decision-making authority. Empathy represents the fundamental capability which separates exceptional leadership from the rest. Actual leadership skill through empathy goes beyond kindness because it means deeply understanding how your team members feel and what they need and see. Such an environment creates trust together with loyalty and collaboration which allows people to experience valuable support.

Leaders who show empathy create upshots of enhanced team productivity along with higher levels of engagement from their workers. Empathetic leaders develop powerful connections with their teams through which they achieve greater teamwork and lower employee stress; according to extensive research. Workers who receive attention from their organization tend to stay committed leading to lasting achievement for personal and business objectives.

Empathetic leaders demonstrate their understanding through the recognition of physical expressions and by paying full attention and creating replies that convey understanding to others. The approach a leader takes when showing empathy towards workplace conflicts and concerns transform how work operates within organizations. This story illustrates both resilience and powerful characteristics produced by insufficient empathy as well as the leadership skills that result from such experiences.

Story: Tough Times Never Last

A farming village supported a farmer who kept a donkey at his place. The former hardworking donkey grew old to the extent that his service became pointless for farm duties. Understanding that his old age rendered him useless for work the farmer allowed him to roam freely in his fields all day.

The donkey ate grass as sunlight shone upon him but unfortunately lost his footing and dropped into a deep long well. As the donkey remained trapped in the well he became petrified while producing desperate loud cries from his frightened state. After a lengthy period of more than 50 minutes, the farmer's adjacent neighbour became able to detect the donkey's loud pleading sounds.

Curiosity along with concern drove him to the well where he discovered the donkey held tightly at the bottom. With no patience, he hurried to the village to deliver the news to the farmer. The farmer learned the news through somebody's voice so he immediately assembled neighbors to bring help for the trapped donkey.

All members of the group ran toward the well where they found the donkey sitting with dejected expressions while his eyes filled with sorrowful tears. The team attempted all sorts of methods they could muster to pull the donkey out of the well, but their efforts were to no avail. The farmer, growing increasingly consumed by a combination of despair and pragmatism as the day advanced, made a heartbreaking decision.

He decided that the donkey was too old and it could be impossible to save him. Determined to follow through, he told his neighbours to fill in the well with dirt and bury the donkey. Reluctantly, the neighbours took up shovels and started tossing dirt into the well.

As the soil started covering him, the donkey's heart fell deeper. Realizing what his master had chosen, he shouted even louder in torment. But with increasing soil pouring over him, a spark of determination arose in him.

Each time a spade of soil fell onto his back, the donkey did something incredible. He tossed off the soil and employed it as a stepping stone to climb higher. Gradually and methodically, he repeated this action, with every layer of soil edging him closer to the summit.

The screams of the donkey eventually stopped after a while, and people who were standing nearby were confused. The farmer also looked into the well, and to his surprise, he noticed the donkey climb onto the heap of dirt that had collected there and elegantly pull itself out of the well. A deep insight hit him as the donkey walked away into the field.

He had learned the reality of his master's affections or the lack of them. With a new sense of freedom and survival, the donkey never looked back, taking his second chance at life. The moral of the story is that difficult times can either hinder you or make you stronger, depending on your reaction.

This is a strong metaphor for leadership. A leader who is not empathetic, such as a farmer, could reject valuable people without realizing their challenges and worth. True leaders, though, such as the donkey, stand taller than adversity, using hardship to propel growth and determination.

Actionable Insights: Using Empathy in Leadership

- Empathy Creates Trust and Loyalty: A listener who cares generates trust. Workers feel secure, trusting that their problems are heard. Trust creates loyalty, decreasing turnover and encouraging a dedicated team. Take a few minutes to check in with your people, ask open-ended questions, and listen carefully.

- Active Listening and Reading Non-Verbal Behaviors: Empathic leaders are more than words. They pay attention to body language, tone, and emotion. If an employee appears disengaged, a leader must approach him or her with inquiry instead of assumption. Rather than responding impulsively, ask, "I have noticed you appear distant today—is there something I can help you with?"
- Replying with Empathy, Not Only Solutions: At times, workers do not require a solution—they require empathy. If someone is explaining a challenge, do not leap to solve the issue right away. Rather, validate their feelings: "That sounds incredibly tough. I'm glad you've shared this with me." Doing so makes people feel heard.

A workplace creates psychological safety which enables workers to share concerns without risking any negative consequences. Leaders can develop psychological safety through their support of open dialogue together with honest mistake recognition and vulnerable leadership conduct. Employees feel connected when their leader states "I don't possess every solution but will tackle problems with you."

The implementation of business decisions results in effects on personnel. The behaviours of an empathetic leader focus on understanding how employee decisions will impact those below them. Employees should be included in decisions leading up to transformational changes across the workplace. 'Please describe to me how this situation will impact you.' Such actions lead to more coordinated progress along with higher employee commitment.

The presence of empathy transforms workplace conflicts into opportunities for enhancement because they exist in all organizations. Leaders should replace blame games with facilitation that allows them to listen to all viewpoints. Through the statement "Help me understand your concerns" leaders can achieve de-escalation that leads to teamwork in creating better solutions.

Employees exhibit leadership qualities which match the behaviour demonstrated by their leaders. Leadership through empathy shows itself in how the leader behaves. Lead by showing your personal experiences and admitting your errors in addition to presenting sincere compassion. Empathetic leadership starts from the top of an organization and then spreads throughout the entire organizational culture.

The act of demonstrating empathy provides leaders with a unique strength that produces outstanding leadership. Leaders who understand others achieve team motivation and organizational success by motivating people who succeed in professional development. Empathetic leaders understand hardship as an opportunity to build resilience and growth through challenges like the donkey used an adverse situation to escape from the well.

Chapter 8. Negotiation Skills: How to Turn No into Yes

The vital life skill of negotiation enables people to open doors which appear completely unmovable. The power to transform negative replies into affirmative responses will determine both your achievements and your business outcomes in all situations. The human talent for negotiation can be learned as an acquired skill which depends on creating strategies and demonstrating patience plus understanding human psychological behaviour.

Effective negotiation requires preparation as its fundamental element. Without prior research, you become unarmed in a negotiation setting similar to starting a battle without military equipment. Every negotiation requires information gathering so you understand what drives the other party. Better control of discussions happens when you possess substantial information about them. Equally vital is objective clarity. Defining your specific negotiation targets alongside establishing essential priorities allows the negotiation process to simplify itself and protects against accepting inferior terms.

Among the core concepts in negotiation exists the Best Alternative to a Negotiated Agreement which is known as BATNA. Having diligent preparation becomes your most advantageous strategy when negotiations end unsuccessfully. Being confident and powerful because of a strong BATNA gives you the capacity to negotiate strong deals without being desperate during transactions. Successful negotiators pursue concepts that benefit each participant so that nobody feels like they come out as the loser. The resulting long-term relationships together with built trust make following negotiations easier.

Here the story of the eagle demonstrates through its actions that negotiation success requires resilience alongside vision and tenacity to achieve impossible outcomes.

Story: The Eagle's Attitude for Success

Long ago, in a thick forest, a wise old eagle lived. The eagle was loved and envied by all other birds due to its immense strength, keen eyesight, and regal demeanour. Numerous young birds wished to be similar to the eagle, but only one dared to approach the eagle for its advice.

One day, a young bird went to the eagle and asked, "You are the best of all. How can I become successful like you?"

The eagle gazed at the young bird and replied, "Success is not luck; it is attitude. If you want to become great, you have to follow the five principles that eagles follow."

The vision was the first lesson. The eagle nudged his nose toward a small rabbit at some distance away in the field and said, "I can spot that rabbit from up here as well. When I place my gaze upon something, I never lose track, regardless of whatever is going on around me. You must keep doing that, too—name your goal and never let your eyes waver from it.

The second lesson was Fearlessness. The eagle went on, "When I go hunting, I do not pay attention to the size of my target. Even if it is larger than I am, I don't hesitate. You have to put up with challenges with the same bravery and never let fear guide your actions.

The third lesson was Tenacity. The eagle explained, "Unlike other birds, when storms arise, I do not take cover. Rather, I embrace the wind, stretch my wings, and soar above the clouds. A good negotiator uses challenges as stepping stones instead of viewing them as obstacles."

The fourth was Resilience. The eagle declared, "There is a moment in my life when I need to moult my old feathers, shatter my beak, and renew them. It hurts, but it makes me resilient. So, in negotiation, you have to be flexible, shed the old ways, and improve.

The fifth and last lesson was Nurturing Relationships. "We eagles care very well for our youngsters so they're healthy enough to fly. Genuine success isn't just winning a single negotiation, but developing enduring relationships.

The young bird paid close attention, learning everything he could. Years went by, and he trained in vision, courage, determination, and tactics. He learned to deal with situations, make bargains, and make a name for himself. Years went by, and he came back to pay thanks to the eagle because all those lessons had changed his life.

The story in a nutshell—is that negotiation is all about attitude, patience, and strategy. If you adopt these beliefs, you will be able to reverse even the most difficult of circumstances in your favour.

Actionable Insights

We now have the mindset necessary for negotiation; now let us learn some step-by-step things you can do to get a 'no' transformed into a 'yes' in your everyday situation.

1. Prepare Thoroughly Before Negotiation

Take time to research before stepping into any negotiation. Learn what the other party cares about, prepare their points of objection, and identify your non-negotiables. Preparation enables you to make valid arguments and advances your likelihood of success.

One of the crucial tools in preparation is the BATNA (Best Alternative to a Negotiated Agreement). When you know your best alternative, then you negotiate knowing when to walk away from the deal if it is not what you want.

2. Create a Clear and Confident Communication Style

Negotiation is a matter of persuading. How you present your offer is significant. Rather than stating, "I require a salary increase," you may state, "Given market conditions and my inputs, I feel that an increase in salary to X amount best represents my contribution to the firm." This takes the discussion away from a demand and towards a logical request.

Active listening is the other key aspect. Listen to the concerns of the other party, recognize them, and then make a counteroffer. This makes the negotiation collaborative and not confrontational.

3. Harness Emotional Intelligence

Excellent negotiators read between the lines—attentive to body language, tone, and emotions. When you notice reluctance, deal with concerns first before making further moves. If the other side is disengaged, pose open-ended questions to get them engaged again.

Using mirroring—repeating key phrases the other person says—creates a subconscious connection. If someone says, "I'm worried about the costs," you can respond, "I understand that cost is a concern. Let's explore options that fit your budget while meeting both our needs."

4. Create a Win-Win Outcome

Negotiation is not about 'winning' by making the other person lose. The best deals are those where both parties feel they've gained something valuable. Find common ground and propose solutions that benefit both sides.

For example, if you're negotiating a contract and the other party is hesitant about pricing, offer added value instead of reducing the price—such as extended service, faster delivery, or customization.

5. Master the Art of Silence and Timing

Silence can be a great tool in negotiations. When you propose, stay silent. Humans feel uneasy with silence and tend to open up or agree with you just to end the pause.

Similarly, knowing when to negotiate is crucial. If the other party is in a hurry, you may have the upper hand. If they seem distracted, it may be better to reschedule.

Negotiation isn't manipulation; it's making both sides better. With the eagle's philosophy in mind—having vision, strength, and grit—and the effective skills of BATNA, emotional intelligence, and active listening, you can take even the firmest 'no' and transform it into an eager 'yes.'

With this skill under your belt, you will not only close stronger, more resilient deals, but also develop firmer, lasting relationships that build your success.

Chapter 9. Resilience in the Face of Rejection

How to Combat Negative Thoughts and Triumph

Life is usually a struggle between our dreams and the internal voices of temptation and self-doubt. Every choice that we make is determined by our thoughts, which guide our actions, habits, and eventually, our fate. The strength of the mind is so powerful—it can create dreams or demolish them with a snap of the fingers. This chapter explores the key topic of managing bad thoughts before they manage us. It discusses how momentary temptations can undo a lifetime of integrity and how awareness can be the secret to a happy life.

Imagine a moment in which one mistake can cost another everything they ever believed in. An individual living a virtuous life, with carelessness, can be swept into the dangers of greed, insecurity, or fear. What we think about is like what we plant in the ground. If we give rise to something good, then we have a garden of plenty, but if we let negative things grow, we can lose ourselves in the jungle of regrets.

The tale below is a strong allegory for how we handle the trials of life. It teaches us that the real test of character is not in one heroic act of honesty but in the mundane choices we make, particularly when nobody is looking.

Story: The Test of Thoughts

A long time ago, Suraj resided in the bustling kingdom with his parents, but they passed when he was still young. He had always known struggle. After losing his parents in early childhood, Suraj spent his days performing various jobs to find sufficient food for survival. Each day proved challenging for him because he managed to make a success sometimes but other times came home with nothing and faced starvation with exhaustion. Honesty represented the limit of his concessions because Suraj never wavered on this principle.

Suraj returned home, exhausted from his failed job searching activities on that lengthy afternoon. An elderly person shouted behind Suraj with a worn-out voice that demanded, "Young man, can you assist me?".

An elderly man stood before him carrying three large distinctive bags which seemed to tax his body. "I have to go to the next village. I can manage two bags, but this third one is too heavy for me. Would you help me carry it? I will give you three gold coins."

Suraj hesitated for a moment but then agreed. "Yes, I can carry it."

He picked up the bag, feeling immediately its weight on his shoulders. He saw the old man observing him wincing and leaned forward to whisper, "That bag is filled with bronze coins, that's why it's so heavy."

Suraj, though tired, began to walk with the old man. While they walked, he could sense how the old man would steal glances at him, looking suspicious. Something occurred to Suraj: He must be thinking that I could steal the bag and run. He was insulted a bit but soon calmed himself. I am not a thief. I am an honest worker.

After having walked for some time, they came to a river. The old man paused on the banks. "I am too old to wade across this river with both bags. Will you take one more?"

Suraj, although exhausted, complied. As he bent down to pick up another bag, the old man placed a warning, "Vow to me that you will not run away. This one is loaded with silver coins.

Suraj scowled. "Do I appear dishonest to you?" he said. "Don't worry, I will take it."

With both bags on his shoulders, he waded through the river. Having reached the other side safely, he turned to see the old man still eyeing him suspiciously. Part of him was annoyed—why was this old man so suspicious?

When they went on further, they encountered a steep slope. The old man panted, finding it impossible to ascend. "Young man, please carry my remaining bag. That one has gold coins in it."

Suraj's temper snapped. "You don't have any faith in me, do you?" he complained. "I have borne two of your bags over a river, but you still question my integrity."

The old man paused before he gave him the third bag. "Proceed. I will take my time coming up. Meet me at the summit."

As Suraj ascended, another idea intruded into his brain. The old man is slow. I would be out of reach if I ran. Three sacks filled with coins—bronze, silver, and gold. I could be set! He struggled to suppress the thought, but it was replaced by another one: He is an old man. What is he going to use all this money for? I could remake my life forever.

His heart raced. His fists gripped the bags. I could live in comfort, get married well, and never have to fight again.

Consumed by greed, Suraj fled. He ran as hard as his legs would carry him until he arrived at his house, panting. Shaking his hands, he opened the first bag—and he gasped. It was packed with pebbles. Baffled, he opened the second—more pebbles. The third—just soil.

There was a letter in the bag. He opened it and trembled as he unfolded it.

"I am the king of this realm. I have no successor. I was looking for a person with integrity to be my successor. Had you fought against your momentary lust, you might have been that man."

Suraj fell to the ground, his heart heavy with the burden of his error. A lifetime of integrity had been undone in a moment of weakness.

Actionable Insights: Mastering Our Thoughts

The lesson that Suraj's story teaches us is one of great value—our biggest battles are the ones we fight in our minds. It is simple to be truthful when there is no temptation, but the real test is when desire and opportunity meet. How do we battle these negative thoughts and win?

1. Identify Negative Thoughts Right Away

Thoughts keep coming up, and not all of them are beneficial to us. The important thing is to recognize negative thoughts as soon as they occur. Suraj's initial negative thought was to run away with the money. If he had realized it was harmful, he could have prevented himself from carrying it out.

2. Challenge the Thought Before Acting on It

After a negative thought occurs, challenge it. Ask yourself:

- Is this idea in accordance with my principles?
- Will this lead to long-term joy or merely short-term success?
- What are the potential outcomes of doing what the idea suggests?

Had Suraj posed these questions, he would have known that it was not what he stood for and that short-term riches would be at the expense of long-term remorse.

3. Reframe the Idea with a Positive Alternative

When in the temptation of negative thinking, counter it with a positive replacement thought. Rather than saying, I can become wealthy overnight by just taking these bags, Suraj could have said to himself, Real success derives from hard work and honesty.

4. Practice Mindfulness and Awareness

Buddha once told us, "Your worst enemy cannot harm you as much as your own unguarded thoughts." Mindfulness helps us notice our mental chatter. Meditation, slow breathing, or just taking a moment before acting can keep us grounded in our values.

5. Seek Guidance and Support

Whenever in doubt, consult mentors, friends, or elders who practice integrity. If Suraj had consulted a wise person about his feelings of temptation, they could have steered him away from the wrong path.

6. See Challenges as Tests of Character

Every difficult situation is an opportunity to prove our strength. Instead of seeing temptation as an obstacle, view it as a test—one that, if passed, will bring greater rewards than giving in ever could.

Thoughts are the designers of our fate. Suraj's story is a reminder that the failure of one moment can override a lifetime of integrity. But by cultivating awareness, second-guessing our desires, and opting for integrity over transient wishes, we can have a life of contentment untainted by regret.

In the end, greatness isn't measured by what we achieve but by how steadfast we remain in the face of temptation. Let us strive to master our thoughts, for in doing so, we master our lives.

Chapter 10. Handling Competitors

In the complex game of professional competition, upholding ethics and integrity is easier said than done. The terrain is teeming with political maneuvers, ruthless tactics, and unrelenting competition, all of which may test one's moral sense. But it is not only possible but necessary for sustained success to remain ethical in these complexities.

Most professionals are presented with situations where the option between short-term returns and long-term credibility is made tough. In the corridors of corporate boardrooms, entrepreneurial setups, or artistic fields, being able to spot and smoothly deal with such political situations is a very important ability. Though some do think that achievement comes with outwitting competitors using dishonesty or trickery, history is not on their side. Entrepreneurs and leaders focusing on ethics and integrity instead tend to create stronger, more enduring brands and relationships.

Building allies in a professional environment does not mean compromising one’s values. Instead, it involves forging genuine relationships, demonstrating reliability, and proving one’s worth through actions rather than words. Keeping integrity intact while handling competitors requires a balance between assertiveness and respect, ensuring that every action taken aligns with a clear ethical framework.

This chapter follows these themes in the inspiring narrative of a blind man in a market place, describing how minor yet reflective alterations in words and actions can produce profound change. It then turns to practical lessons on how professionals can maintain ethics amidst the competitive landscape.

The Power of Words

One day, in a crowded marketplace, an elderly blind man sat at the side of an alley, his weak hands lying next to an empty hat containing but a few scattered coins. Next to him, a signboard bore the inscription, "I am blind. Please help me." Ordinary people continued walking without contribution as they passed through the crowd.

The young female worker on her way to work noticed the elderly man amid moving people in the rush hour. The woman briefly explored her bag before she placed her small coins into the hat collection. She glanced at the signboard as she made her departure. There was something wrong with the sign which perhaps made it mediocre to the point of disappearing from attention.

Her eyes traveled between the scene and the signboard before she took the writing tool to rewrite something that caught her attention. She placed the signboard in its position to appeal to every person who walked by. She continued her journey to work with a pleasant expression on her face as she didn't realize she was setting off a great reaction with her words.

As the day went on, something amazing occurred. Increasingly, people stopped next to the old man. Some looked at the sign, smiled, and without a moment's hesitation, deposited coins into his hat. Others paused for a moment to say something kind or give him a pat on the back. The previously empty hat started filling up, the clinking metallic sound of coins against one another increasing.

That afternoon, when the young woman walked back home, the blind man recognized her footsteps. He slightly turned his head in her direction and inquired, "Excuse me, were you the one who altered my sign this morning? My hat has been full all day! What did you write?"

She knelt down next to him, her eyes warm with gentleness. "I only wrote the truth," she said. "You wrote, 'I am blind. Help me.' I rewrote it as, 'It is a beautiful day, and I can't see it.'"

There was a moment of silence between them. Then, a smile creased the old man's face. He got it. It was not just what was said—how they were said, what feelings they called up.

Words, after all, are more than just sounds or letters. They shape our thoughts, influence our actions, and change the course of our lives. The woman's carefully chosen words didn't just describe the blind man's condition; they made passersby feel something. Instead of stating a fact, the new sign evoked empathy, prompting them to act.

Similar to the tale of the blind man, business professionals working in competitive industries can easily fall short of using effective communication that avoids hurting others. The manner of communication we exhibit, be it in negotiations within a business setup, market campaign, or corporate leadership, establishes how others interact with us. It is not what you speak, but the way you do it.

Language evokes mental images and feelings. The proper use of words can ignite loyalty, generate trust, and build long-term professional partnerships, but careless or deceitful words can ruin reputations and cut off opportunities. Just as the young woman's humble rephrasing changed the old man's destiny, leaders and professionals can frame their own success by recognizing the power of communication and moral interactions.

Actionable Insights

The story of the blind man highlights a powerful lesson: the right words, framed ethically and empathetically, can change outcomes. This principle applies directly to handling competitors in professional settings. Here are key actionable insights on staying ethical amidst professional complexities:

1. Recognizing Political Dynamics Without Compromising Values

Every professional environment has its own unspoken rules, alliances, and power structures. Understanding these dynamics is crucial for making informed decisions.

But to recognize politics does not equate to unethical behavior. Rather, observe, analyze, and answer strategically with integrity.

In the presence of office politics or competitive rivalries, emphasize open communication and truthful performance over sneaky methods.

2. The Power of Ethical Framing

As the young woman's shift in wording resulted in more compassion, how we frame ourselves and our work does matter.

Rather than pointing out competitors' weaknesses, focus on the strengths and special value your work offers.

Ethical framing establishes credibility. In the long term, companies and professionals with a reputation for integrity draw higher-quality partnerships and opportunities.

3. Creating Allies Through Authentic Relationships

In a competitive marketplace, solid relationships can be the determining factor. But these alliances need to be founded on trust, not manipulation.

Help coworkers and competitors equally when fairness demands. A reputation makes an individual a renowned figure in any profession.

Networking must be about mutual growth, joint knowledge, and value creation and not just self-interest.

4. Ethics as Competitive Strength

Professionals find that shortcuts and competitive aggression ensure success. Nonetheless, ethical actions often create solid long-term gains.

Businesses and individuals with integrity draw investors, customers, and staff who appreciate honest behavior, and with that, sustainable growth.

When ever confronted by a choice between short-term profit and long-term trust, opt for trust. Reputation once lost is difficult to restore.

5. Managing Rivalries with Diplomacy

Good competition fuels growth, while unethical competition generates toxicity. Treat competitors as fellow professionals and not as enemies.

When adversaries attempt to undermine you, be professional, not retaliatory. Frequently, patience and persistent ethical behavior outlast devious behavior.

Victories should be celebrated modestly and losses gracefully. The power to hold dignity in both situations enhances credibility.

6. Exercising Ethical Influence

Words have an impact on perception. Ethical persuasion centers on truth, simplicity, and compassion instead of manipulation.

Whether selling an idea, managing a team, or mediating conflicts, positive language can motivate collaboration over conflict.

Authenticity creates stronger personal and professional reputations. People are more inclined to follow leaders who speak clearly and honestly.

In the high-stakes arena of professional competition, the allure to shave the edges off ethics can be great. But the blind man's tale is a reminder that words and deeds, when established with integrity and thoughtfulness, carry the power to alter results. Success founded on ethics, trust, and moral impact endures over time.

By seeing political dynamics without being controlled by them, establishing real relationships, and speaking wisely, professionals can work through competition while maintaining their values. The secret is to keep in mind that ethical success isn't merely about winning—it's about winning with integrity. And ultimately, that's the type of victory that really counts.

Chapter 11. Positive Attitude

Positive and negative attitudes are two sides of the same coin—what we decide to cultivate decides the direction of our life. A positive attitude is not something that occurs overnight; it is developed over time through small, persistent good habits. These habits, if done regularly, become strongly embedded in our subconscious and influence our behavior, mindset, and eventually, our destiny. An individual with a positive attitude tends to find happiness and success as natural consequences of their disciplined life.

To develop a positive attitude, one needs to consciously take up and practice values like optimism, resilience, empathy, and a growth mindset. These are not one-off tasks but consistent practices undertaken on a daily basis, which gradually change our view of life.

Suppose there is a room in which three young people are seated side by side. The first young person is good-natured, fit, attends the gym, reads positive books, and consumes a healthy diet. With the passage of time, these practices make him build a robust, positive personality. Next to him sits the third young person—an addict and chain smoker who consumes a lot of dirty street food and has tuberculosis because of neglect and wrong decisions.

Now look at the second person, who is seated between them. He is a choice. If he wants to be like the first youth, he has to embrace discipline, eat healthy, and always practice good habits. But if he wants to be like the third, he has to do nothing—negativity tends to spread without effort. Even a mere cough from the third person can infect him. This demonstrates a deep truth: one doesn't have to do hard work in order to get into negativity, but becoming a positive individual is a conscious process and practice each day.

Then, think positive, act positive, and enjoy a life filled with happiness and success.

Life is unpredictable. Change is inevitable. Persons who wish to handle life's constant transformations need adaptability as their primary navigational tool. Human beings often fight against change because they lack familiarity with the unknown aspects of upcoming modifications. People resist change because they experience negative thoughts along with future uncertainties and doubts about their abilities and concerns about future setbacks. Eagerly accepting change through optimistic thinking enables people to extract beneficial growth from demanding scenarios.

When dealing with changes proactively one must prepare ahead of time engage openly with others and maintain a positive mental state. Ready to accept life's changes comes from preparedness for their possibility. Open communication provides us with necessary support from the people we surround ourselves with. The most powerful quality of a positive attitude allows people to solve challenges and see open doors despite obstacles.

Our thoughts exert an extremely powerful effect on everything. Thoughts shape our understanding of events while guiding our choices until they determine our end results in life. Negative thoughts that gain entry into our minds can eventually lead to feelings of regret about what we might have accomplished. Through positive thinking we secure the path to achievement and create space for happiness and the ability to overcome challenges that come our way. This story presents an example that shows that losing one's mindset brings permanent consequences.

The Power of Positive Attitude

Many years ago, there were two adjacent kingdoms on the verge of conflict. One was a huge, mighty empire with a ten-fold larger army. The other kingdom was smaller, already accepting that they would be defeated. They understood that victory was impossible and their generals feared that their troops were not strong enough to oppose the enemy forces.

Awe held the soldiers, and even the king began to doubt his chances. Some counsellors even proposed surrendering before the battle could start.

But the king, though knowing of their disadvantage, was not prepared to give up. He was a brave man who thought that a battle should be fought with determination and not with fear. Having seen his generals hesitate, he consulted with a respected monk who dwelled in a village in his kingdom. The monk was highly respected for his sagacity and had guided the folk through troubles many times before.

The king told him of his problem, hoping for a suggestion on how to change things. The monk listened thoughtfully and then, to the amazement of the king, said, "Appoint me as commander of your armies."

The king was hesitant. "But, Master, you have never been in war. How can you command my troops?"

The monk smiled. "War is not merely swords and men; it is about the power of the mind. Believe me, and we will fight."

Having complete trust in the monk, the king commissioned him as commander. Word got around the kingdom, and the soldiers, who were already disappointed, became more fearful.

A monk, never having wielded a sword before, was now to take them into battle? Still, there was nothing to do but comply.

As they went to the battlefield, they crossed a small temple. The monk stopped and addressed the army. "Before we go into battle, let us seek the Almighty's guidance. We shall ask whether we are destined to win or lose. If the divine forces indicate defeat, we shall retreat. But if they assure us of victory, we shall march forward fearlessly."

Even sceptical, the soldiers nodded in agreement. The monk folded his hands in a prayer, and then produced a coin from his pocket. "I will flip this coin. If it falls heads, it is sure that we will win. And if it falls tails, it is that we have to go back."

Holding their breath, the soldiers watched as the monk tossed the coin high into the air. It spun and landed on the ground—heads up. The monk raised his arms and proclaimed, "The Almighty has spoken! Victory is ours! Now, let us fight with all our strength!"

The soldiers, seeing what they believed to be a divine sign, were filled with new energy. Their fear disappeared, replaced by an unshakable belief in victory. With newfound confidence, they charged into battle against the mighty enemy.

The battle was fierce, but the smaller army fought with extraordinary bravery. With the fervent belief that they were destined to triumph, they overwhelmed their adversaries. In the end, the erstwhile mighty enemy was vanquished, and the smaller kingdom triumphed.

On their return journey, the monk again took the troops to the temple. "Let us thank the Almighty for our triumph!" The soldiers zealously thanked him.

Then the monk took out the coin and displayed it to them. "Before you thank the Almighty, look at this coin." The soldiers gasped in shock—it was a double-headed coin! Regardless of how it was thrown, it could never fall on tails.

The monk replied, "Don't thank fate for your triumph. You won because you believed in yourselves. As soon as you believed victory was certain, you fought with your entire heart. Had you gone to war expecting to lose, you certainly would have."

The soldiers realized the real lesson: the strength of faith and optimism had brought them victory. The monk went on, "In life, success is not only a matter of our ability but of our attitude. Those who are positive thinkers and have faith in themselves can do the impossible. It is not merely talent that leads to success but the faith and commitment one puts into their endeavors."

Actionable Insights from the Story

Self-Belief Shapes Reality

The coin trick of the monk illustrates how belief influences results. Individuals who believe in themselves act with confidence, resulting in success. Doubt may result in fear and failure. To foster self-confidence, imagine success and tackle obstacles with perseverance. Recount past successes to build positive thoughts.

Fear Weakens, Positivity Strengthens

The soldiers initially feared the battle because they assumed defeat. Fear drains energy and clouds judgment, whereas optimism fuels courage and resilience. When facing difficulties, replace fear with positive affirmations. Instead of "I can't do this," say, "I will find a way to succeed." Surround yourself with supportive influences to maintain positivity.

Mindset is More Powerful than Circumstances

The army of the smaller kingdom was outnumbered, but they triumphed since their attitude changed. This holds true for challenges in real life—be it professional, personal, or even in relationships. Instead of dwelling on problems, reinterpret challenges as a chance to grow. Stay with a growth mindset and transform setbacks into learning opportunities.

A Leader's Confidence Inspires Others

The monk's unwavering confidence affected an entire army. Leaders who radiate optimism and self-confidence can turnaround teams, businesses, or communities. If you're in a leadership role, instill confidence by staying calm in times of crisis. Lead the way, exhibiting strength and an unshakeable belief in achievement.

Take Bold Steps with Conviction

The monk did not hesitate when commanded, and he found a means to give faith to the soldiers. Individuals who take firm action are likely to be successful, even when they have no resources or experience. Rather than think through risks excessively, take deliberate steps ahead. Have faith in your skills, give it your best shot, and victory will be yours.

In the end, this tale reminds us that positive thinking holds the power to shape our fates. In war or in life, our attitude is what achieves. Have faith in yourself, accept obstacles, and triumph will be yours.

Chapter 12. Stress Management and Wellness

Introduction to the Theme

In this fast pace of life, where professional stresses, deadlines, and personal concerns always compete with each other on priority, stress is an inevitability in life. Most professionals tend to overdo, prioritizing work over health and reaching the state of utter exhaustion, both physically as well as mentally. The twist in the circumstance is that even while careers and ambitions provide a sense of accomplishment, they accomplish this at the cost of well-being. This imbalance can lead to burnout, anxiety, and even long-term health problems if not managed well.

Stress, if not addressed and controlled in the early stages, may seep into all walks of life. Relationships get affected, work suffers, and even the smallest tasks begin to feel insurmountable. The trick is to know how to put first things first—how to ensure that health, family, and personal contentment are not being traded off for short-term career success.

This chapter delves into a compelling analogy that illustrates how to balance the duties of life astutely. By prioritizing what matters, one can continue to live a satisfying life and still thrive in a high-stress profession. A tale of a philosophy professor and his humble but enlightening experiment with a jar, stones, pebbles, sand, and water provides a metaphor for coping with stress and well-being. It brings out the significance of prioritizing, the balance between work and life, and the fact that stress does not overshadow life's real joys.

In this story, we'll learn real strategies to fight back against stress—mindfulness, exercise, and establishing work-life boundaries. We'll also explore how early signs of burnout can prompt one to take preventative measures before stress becomes serious. Life is more than getting work done and setting goals; life is about having room for what matters in terms of happiness, satisfaction, and inner peace.

Let's read this thought-provoking story that will revolutionize the way you think about stress and balance in life.

Read this...

There was one day when a local philosophy professor, who was famous for his unique teaching approach, paid a special visit to an elementary school. He was always interactive and philosophical in his approach to teaching, making his students learn life lessons in the most memorable ways.

When he arrived on the day of his visit, he walked into a crowded classroom with a curious twinkle in his eyes and a big, empty glass jar under his arm. The students' interest was immediately sparked. With a sense of mischievous intrigue, it was clear that this would not be a typical school day.

He put the jar down in the center of the room facing the class and went under the table to pick up a handful of huge stones, about the size of one's fist. He very deliberately started dropping them into the jar, each individual stone, until he couldn't add anymore. He looked around at the class and inquired, "Is this jar full?"

The students, observing that no more stones could be added, nodded vigorously and answered, "Yes."

The professor, with a smile, brought out a pouch of pebbles and began to pour them into the jar, giving it a slight shake. The pebbles, much smaller than the stones, rolled into the available space among the stones. He once more asked the class, "Is the jar full now?"

A few students, who were finally starting to get his message, hesitated, but most still answered, "Yes, now it's full."

The professor next pulled out a bag of sand and poured it into the jar very slowly. The small grains dripped down, filling up the small crevices between the pebbles and stones. He once again asked, "Is the jar full now?"

The students, by this point, had realized his point. They hesitated, then said, "Probably not."

Nodding, the professor got up and fetched a jug of water, which he poured into the jar and filled the sand. Only after that did he assent, "Yes, now the jar is full."

He turned to survey the room, where his young audience wore puzzled, enlightened faces. Then he explained, "I want you to understand that this jar symbolizes your life."

The big rocks are the most significant things—your family, your health, your dreams. If all else were gone and only they were left, your life would still be rich and worthwhile."

"The pebbles are the other important things—your job, your home, your car. They are valuable but secondary to the big rocks.

The sand symbolizes the little things—the daily tasks, petty concerns, and undue stress. If you pack your jar with sand or pebbles first, there won't be room for the big stones."

He paused and continued, "This is exactly how life works. If you spend all your time and energy on the small things—answering emails, running errands, obsessing over minor problems—you'll never have space for what truly matters. Prioritize the large stones first. Everything else will fall into place."

Just as he finished, a thoughtful student raised her hand and asked, "Professor, what about the water?"

He smiled, acknowledging her perceptive question. "Ah, the water! The water represents that however full life may appear to be, there is always space for a cup of tea or coffee with a friend. There is always room for laughter, relaxation, and little moments of happiness."

The class sank into reflective silence as the students absorbed the deeper lesson. The experiment was a straightforward demonstration, but it held a lifetime's worth of wisdom.

In this analogy, the professor indirectly taught one of the most important lessons regarding stress management and wellness: prioritize what is most important, set boundaries, and never allow the little worries to overwhelm the big pleasures.

Actionable Insights

1. Prioritize Your Stones First

Determine what is most important in your life. Your health, family, and personal goals must always take precedence over workday stressors. If you do not prioritize them, you will regret it in the future. Make sure that your calendar represents your actual priorities.

2. Recognize and Control Stress Early

Over time stress builds up progressively which makes it easy to miss its development until it becomes overwhelming. Start early intervention by watching for burnout warning signs which include persistent tiredness together with irritability and difficulty concentrating. Daily integration of stress reduction elements including deep breathing exercises and self-evaluation and short breaks should be a permanent part of your lifestyle.

3. Add Mindfulness and Exercise

The practice of mindfulness includes meditation together with journaling appreciation and deep breathing to ground you in the present moment. Daily walking serves as an excellent practice for reducing stress. The activities provide you with tools to develop better resistance against ordinary stressors.

4. Establish Work-Life Boundaries

Employees who work stressful jobs often find it difficult to draw boundaries which prevent their personal life from mingling with work responsibilities. Everyday activities outside the workplace must be Endless block during specific times and moving away from work-related obligations like email-checking. Also allows complete personal downtime without interruptions. Establishing this balance between work and personal life serves to minimize the stress that flows from work into your environment.

5. Create Space for Enthusiasm and Relationships

The professor used water analogies in his lesson indicating that happiness together with rest are essential lifestyle components. You can restore your emotional balance through multiple restorative activities including conversations with friends, recreational hobbies and watching daytime sunsets.

Using the described strategies will help you maintain career achievement as well as personal wellness so stress cannot dominate important life aspects.

Chapter 13. Leading by Example

Introduction to the Theme

True leadership requires action with integrity, together with the ability to influence others above conventional authority and positions of power. True leaders avoid commanding others because their deeds serve as inspiration to others. They start by demonstrating the same values which they expect their team members to display. An organization and community thrive when leadership demonstrates by example because this approach creates credibility and trust and builds motivation, which together establish the essential foundation for all organizational success.

Consistent conduct between words and actions makes individuals look up to human beings as natural leaders. The most valuable leaders show their example first by persisting and demonstrating high moral values while working for excellence. Deeds surpass words in every aspec,t including both work and home environment and within social circles. Human credibility as a leader can only be measured through authentic actions and not through empty declarations.

Leaders lose their credibility whenever they say something but fail to accomplish those things themselves. Visualize an authority figure who maintains tight deadlines but misses all deadlines or a person who requires discipline while coming in late too frequently. Such behavior leads to nothing but anger instead of gaining respect from others. Through physical involvement with his team to overcome challenges, leaders build teams that bring out responsibility and committed performance.

The most influential global leaders, including Gandhi and Mandela and Lincoln created their roles through their genuine embodiment of their core values rather than their speaking abilities. Through their real-world conduct these leaders established their leadership while creating worldwide movements for change.

Lasting credibility stands as a prime necessity in our current fast-moving world, so leading through personal conduct remains the most vital leadership approach. The practice of demonstrating your values directly results in high standards of accountability, which leads to productive cultural norms and exceptional performance from team members. The upcoming story will show you that genuine leadership appears through real acts instead of verbal statements when it operates in its most basic and impactful form.

The Story

There was a rich kingdom, and in this kingdom lived a wise and good king named Varun. People loved him as he was so fair and compassionate and had the deepest understanding of human nature. Unlike most other rulers who would rule from within their palaces, King Varun would regularly walk around in the kingdom, incognito, eager to know for himself about the lives of his people.

He had a plan one day and conducted a test of sorts to discover how his subjects would behave under adversity. He commanded that a huge boulder be dropped on the middle of the busiest highway leading to the capital. And he waited discreetly close by to note what happened to people as they saw the obstruction.

A well-to-do merchant was the first to reach there. He wore rich silks and was seated comfortably in a sumptuous carriage. When his horses stopped in front of the boulder, the merchant leaned out and glared. "What sort of kingdom lets the roads be closed like this? This is unacceptable! The king should make his laborers remove the roadblock!" he growled. On that, he instructed his carriage to go another way, refusing to get his hands dirty.

Soon, a procession of nobles rode up. They also noticed the boulder and immediately started arguing about who should be made to move it. "The city men should do this!" one of them stated. "We pay taxes for such purposes!" cried another. Following some grumbling, they also rode around the boulder and went on their way.

A few others walked by, such as merchants, soldiers, and officials. All complained, some going so far as to curse the king's government, but none of them tried to roll the boulder.

As the afternoon passed, a peasant named Ravi walked up. He was a farmer, with a heavy bag of vegetables slung over his shoulder, his feet covered in dust from the long trek. Ravi did not complain like the others. He dropped his sack, mopped his brow, and examined the rock. He heaved against it with every ounce of strength, but it did not move. Unfaltering, he pushed once more, using a stick as a fulcrum. Gradually, he inched the boulder onto the road's side.

Weary but content, Ravi lifted his sack and was going to proceed when he saw a small leather pouch where the boulder had rested. Intrigued, he opened it and discovered gold coins and a handwritten message.

"To the one who removes the obstacle, great rewards lie in store. True leaders are not those who lament about problems but those who remove them. — King Varun."

Tears welled up in Ravi's eyes. He never expected a reward—he had moved the boulder simply because it was the right thing to do.

At that time, King Varun came out of his hiding place. "Ravi, today you have shown this kingdom a good lesson. Many went past this rock, grumbling, waiting for someone else to do something. But you, a humble farmer, showed the real spirit of leadership. You acted instead of waiting for others."

The next day, King Varun shared Ravi's story with the kingdom. He addressed his people: "Leadership is not about rank or wealth; it is about setting an example. It is easy to criticize and expect others to act. But the true mark of a leader takes initiative, no matter how small the task."

Inspired by Ravi's act, the kingdom witnessed a shift in attitude. Merchants, nobles, and common folk alike started taking personal responsibility for their surroundings. Streets became cleaner, people helped one another, and a sense of unity flourished.

Ravi, once an ordinary farmer, became an advisor to the king, teaching others that leadership is not about words but about action.

Actionable Insights

1. Walk the Talk

Leaders earn respect and trust if what they do is consistent with what they say. If you want punctuality, be punctual. If you believe in hard work, practice it yourself. The most effective leaders do not direct from the sidelines; they participate actively.

2. Take Responsibility Rather Than Complain

Most individuals recognize issues, but few step up to address them. In the face of challenges, rather than complaining about situations or blaming other people, reflect on yourself and ask, "What can I do to make things better here?" Excellent leaders succeed by taking responsibility.

3. Power Through Small Actions

Leadership doesn't necessarily mean big actions. Small, regular actions—such as assisting a fellow worker, upholding high ethical standards, or owning up to errors—generate a strong ripple effect. If you always behave in a way that shows integrity, others will do the same.

4. Establish Credibility Through Consistency

Consistency can limit leadership when it hinders adaptability. If you preach about work-life balance yet spend every night at the office, your message becomes meaningless. To establish credibility, be what you preach and show consistency over time.

5. Foster a Culture of Initiative

A society or workplace flourishes when people own their problems. Leaders need to identify and reward people who take initiative, as King Varun did to Ravi. Encouragement creates a positive environment where individuals feel motivated to act.

6. Serve Before You Lead

The greatest leaders serve others. They listen to, encourage, and support others. Leadership is about helping others grow, giving them opportunities, and making sure others succeed.

7. Recognize That Leadership Is a Choice, Not a Title

Anyone can be a leader, regardless of position. Whether you're a CEO, teacher, parent, or student, your actions influence others. Leadership is not about waiting for authority—it is about choosing to act responsibly.

Leadership is not quantified by the number of followers but by the number of individuals one motivates to act. Ravi and King Varun's story reminds us that leading by example is the strongest leadership. Each day offers chances to be an example—be it at work, at home, or in the community. The decision to lead begins with us, and it begins with our actions, not our words.

Chapter 14. Nurturing Team Success

Introduction to the Theme

Leadership is usually gauged in terms of individual success, but genuine success is in the development of the team one leads. Excellent leaders guide others but also spark in their followers the ability to shine. Leadership becomes most evident when someone uses their abilities successfully to develop others around them.

Leadership emerges through motivating and empowering everyone to showcase their strengths in their team. The path to achieving top success in our culture of individual congratulation runs through group achievement. History remembers its most legendary figures through their ability to motivate their teams along with developing their followers into leaders beyond their time.

Empowering a team requires more than simple work delegation because it builds an environment which respects and develops all members to maintain their drive for contribution. A leader must both see the particular strengths in team members and help those abilities grow.

From this chapter, we will understand the idea of developing team success by beginning with an allegorical narrative that conveys the essence of resilience, learning from difficulties, and the role of a facilitating environment. We will learn from this story how difficulties, as opposed to roadblocks, are the key to becoming greater. Next, we will take away useful learnings that will enable leaders to apply these in practical contexts.

Story: Obstacles Are a Blessing in Disguise – Overcoming Challenges

There was once a boy named Arjun who lived in a small town. He would spend his summers at his grandfather's place, playing in the fields all day, hearing tales, and learning the old man's wisdom. His grandfather, a wise and respected farmer, had a special method of imparting life lessons through nature.

Arjun once went to his grandfather one summer and said, "Grandpa, when I become big, I want to succeed. Tell me the secret to success."

His grandfather smiled and replied, "Sure, my child, but first, let's conduct an experiment."

Next morning, they went to a nursery and got two small plants. Grandfather planted one in a big pot in the home and the other in the open ground outside.

"What do you think, Arjun? Which plant will grow better?" the old man asked.

Arjun thought for a moment and replied, "The one inside the house, of course! It will be safe from strong winds, heavy rain, and animals. The one outside has to fight so many challenges."

His grandfather simply nodded. "Let's see what happens in a few years."

Years went by, and Arjun went back to his grandfather's home. His first stop with his grandfather was to view the plants.

The plant inside the house had developed, but not much in height. Its branches were frail, and it leaned towards one side, trying hard to carry its own weight. The other outside had grown. Its roots had sunk deep into the ground, and its branches had spread far and wide, casting shadows. It had weathered storms, torrential rains, and intense sunlight—but rather than breaking, it had learned to bend and become strong.

Grandfather smiled at Arjun, "Do you see what occurred? The plant in the house was sheltered, but in doing so, it was not strong. The one outside struggled, but it was those struggles that made it stronger."

His grandfather explained to Arjun that life operates identically. Choosing only easy routes provides short-term protection while preventing your development into being strong. Success comes to those who welcome difficulties and transformation to build a stronger existence. Success will come to those who choose hardship learning as an opportunity for growth.

From where he stood Arjun honored the tree outside. There was no doubt in the message: every challenge functions as a stepping stone which leads to great achievements.

This metaphor provides an excellent model for understanding team building as well as leadership practices. Both the open-field tree and collective groups of people progress in toughness because they face challenges alongside each other. The top-performing teams do not avoid challenges but rather overcome these obstacles to gain knowledge and emergence stronger than before.

Actionable Insights: Applying Leadership Lessons in Team Growth

Emphasize Challenges, Not Comfort

Leaders feel that their teams should be protected from obstacles, expecting ease to achieve success. However, similar to the plant which blossomed in the outdoors, true strength resides in overcoming obstacles and challenges. Inviting teammates outside of the comfort zone to stretch and move encourages resilience as well as innovative thinking.

Application: Rather than providing a solution to all problems yourself, lead them to create solutions by themselves. Give them ownership of important tasks and have faith in their capabilities.

Give the Right Support, Not Protection

A leader does not take away obstacles but gives the team the tools and the confidence to overcome them. As a gardener would tend plants, a leader needs to foster growth by giving them the tools and the support while letting team members adjust to challenges.

Application: Give mentorship, training, and resources that enable your team instead of protecting them from all obstacles.

Identify and Cultivate Personal Strengths

Individuals on each team possess particular strengths. Some individuals may perform their best under crisis situations, and others are outstanding planners and executives. Identifying these strengths and placing individuals into positions where their strengths are developed creates a solid, efficient team.

Application: Hold frequent individual conversations to recognize each team member's goals, strengths, and weaknesses. Provide opportunities that allow them to contribute in areas best suited to their skills and aims.

Develop a Growth Mindset

High-performing teams view obstacles as opportunities to learn rather than as setbacks. Just like the outside plant became stronger by learning to cope with adversity, a feedback-positive, obstacle-as-a-learning-moment team will continue to get stronger.

Implementation: Establish an environment where feedback is positive and appreciated. Provide space for innovation and tolerate mistakes so that lessons are learned and utilized.

Lead by Example

A leader who shows resilience and a desire to overcome obstacles is going to encourage the same from their team. If you want your team to be flexible and motivated, you need to practice these traits yourself.

Application: Demonstrate to your team that you are not afraid to take risks, bend with change, and confront obstacles with confidence. Your actions will motivate them more than words ever could.

Build Collaboration and Support

A supportive team is more powerful than one where individuals work independently. Just like the tree's solid roots created stability, a well-supported team with strong relationships can face any obstacle together.

Application: Build teamwork through group projects, open communication, and peer support. Make the environment conducive to the team members' ability to share ideas freely and request assistance.

Celebrate Growth and AchievementsJust as the tree outside the window came to be a strong, flourishing entity, so will a nurtured team. Acknowledgment of progress and celebrating small achievements keeps motivation in high gear and promotes a culture of ongoing improvement.

Application: Acknowledge milestones, large and small. Periodically appreciate the efforts and express gratitude for individual and team achievements.

Leadership is not about personal glory; it's about the team's success. A successful leader knows that challenges are only growth, not only personally but also as a group. Through creating a culture where members feel motivated to accept adversity, guided in their growth, and enabled to use their strengths to their advantage, leaders set the stage for sustainable success.

Just as the resilient tree that bloomed in the open pasture, the most powerful teams are the ones that encounter challenges, grow, and come out more robust. To create a team that can stand tall, provide them with room to flourish, with the boldness to confront challenges, and the direction to thrive. That is the real mark of a leader's triumph.

Chapter 15. The Value of Lifelong Learning

Introduction to the Theme

Knowledge functions as survival since our world is continuously changing today. Fast technological advancements alongside continuous methodology enhancements and arriving challenges force people to continue learning throughout their lives. Modern professional success no longer depends on stable expertise because lifelong learning itself became one of the main requirements to maintain professional relevance.

The secret to learning throughout your entire life rests in your curiosity. Curiosity drives the development of knowledge and guarantees that innovation continues to progress in the future. The highest-performing leaders, alongside successful individuals, possess a learning mindset because they continuously ask questions while investigating new possibilities to better themselves. No person can succeed by using outdated knowledge because needs transform from day to day. The ability to adapt, to acquire new skills, and to apply knowledge in innovative ways separates leaders from followers, pioneers from the complacent.

In addition, lifelong learning is not limited to formal schooling. Although degrees and diplomas can impart basic know-how, real learning goes far beyond educational environments. It is an attitude that involves reading extensively, discussing matters, experimenting with novel concepts, and practicing what one has learned on the job. The process demands that person question their beliefs so they can gain from their errors and strengthen their knowledge base with experience.

The significance of continuous learning remains critical because artificial intelligence automation and digital transformation are revolutionizing current business industries. Technological acquisition and implementation of better problem-solving approaches and knowledge transfer from others all contribute to significant professional and personal development.

This chapter examines the revolutionary potential of lifelong learning using an engaging anecdote, which demonstrates how staying persistent in learning unlocks the doors to novel possibilities. Last but not least, it offers practical advice on how to create a personal learning roadmap, such that one is nimble and on top of the game in an evolving world.

Story

A long time ago, in a kingdom between great mountains and running rivers, there was a young scholar named Arun. Unlike the conventional scholars who stayed within royal libraries, Arun was fascinated by the world around him and not only within books. According to him, wisdom was not only in books but everywhere in the world.

Then came a critical moment in the life of the kingdom. The main river's water had suddenly begun to stop flowing, and all the fields lay parched while the people worried. The king called in his finest engineers and scholars to see if they could solve the puzzle. They looked at their books of old knowledge, compared outdated engineering blueprints, and discussed for days, but were unable to find the root of the matter.

Arun, also curious, was the exception. Not wanting to waste time, he set out toward the riverhead in the hills. He got his gear in order and made the journey to find out why the river had stopped flowing. Arun encountered an old hermit who resided on the riverside. Finding Arun fascinated, the old hermit greeted him and posed a question to him: "Why do you look for the river's secret?"

"The kingdom is at risk," Arun responded. "If we don't discover the cause of the river's vanishing, our people will perish."

The hermit smiled. "Knowledge isn't only contained in scrolls and conversation. It is concealed in nature, in experience, in the desire to venture beyond what is known." He took Arun higher on the mountain, where they discovered a massive boulder obstructing the flow of the river. "This is your answer," said the hermit.

Arun understood that none of the scholars had thought to look beyond their books. Their intelligence was not in question; rather, they resisted stepping beyond the familiarity of their preferred sources of information. Arun, resolved to fix the issue, assembled villagers from surrounding villages. With immense effort, they battered away at the boulder, eventually breaking it into fragments that could be relocated. As the water flowed once more, Arun experienced a deep sense of satisfaction.

When he arrived back in the kingdom, its people welcomed him as a hero. The king, who was impressed by his initiative, appointed Arun his chief advisor. "You have shown," exclaimed the king, "that knowledge is not merely knowing everything, but seeking solutions with persistence."

Years went by, and Arun's desire to learn never diminished. He brought in new irrigation methods, learned medicine from far-off places, and even picked up foreign languages to promote diplomacy. With every new knowledge he adopted, the kingdom prospered even more.

A young student approached Arun to ask him about the key to his achievements.

Arun responded with a smile while he told the student, "Never believe you have mastered everything." Your mentality of learning stops only when your capacity to advance does. You should always ask questions from every teaching source because learning benefits you throughout your entire existence.

Actionable Insights

1. Adopt a Growth Mindset

The growth mindset teaches people that determination and focused work enable the development of talents and intellectual skills. People embracing this mindset become more resistant to defeat while maintaining an open attitude toward challenges and remain receptive to gain knowledge from mistakes. Learning happens in a perpetual way so treat each setback as an opportunity to develop rather than treating it as something that stands in your path.

2. Conducting Ability to Track Modern Technological Developments and Methodological Approaches

Rapid changes in the world demand strict attention to remain informed. Maintain knowledge growth by reading field updates and taking classes and attending educational events online. Self-directed learners can use the online educational platforms Coursera together with Udemy and LinkedIn Learning for developing their knowledge across multiple disciplines from any location. Tyger children maintain their market relevance through tracking industry trends as well as preventing technological obsolescence.

3. Develop a Personal Learning Roadmap

To make lifelong learning effective, create a structured plan:

Identify Key Areas of Interest: Prioritize skills that fit your goals and interests.

Set Learning Goals: Divide them into short-term and long-term goals.

Allocate Dedicated Time: It may be an hour a day or a few hours a week, but it must be consistent.

Use a Variety of Learning Methods: Read books, listen to podcasts, watch TED talks, and do hands-on experiences.

Track Your Progress: Think about what you have learned and how it has helped you develop.

4. Learn from People and Experiences

Learning is not just in books and classes; it is also in dialogue, observation, and actual experiences. Be with different thinkers, discuss ideas meaningfully, and listen to new ideas. Networking and mentorship are key in continuous learning.

5. Develop a Reading and Writing Habit

Reading broadens the mind, whereas writing clarifies thoughts. Form a reading habit of books, articles, and research reports. Keep a journal or a blog to verbalize your learnings, observations, and musings. Such an exercise not only reinforces memorization but also improves critical thinking abilities.

6. Try Things Out and Use What You Have Learned

Theory is useful, but its full strength is found in application. Whether it is a new programming language, a business tactic, or a creative technique, application makes it stick. Challenge yourself to implement new information in real-world applications.

7. Be Curious and Open-Minded

Curiosity is the spark of lifelong learning. Question, challenge assumptions, and venture beyond your comfort zone. Develop an attitude of openness to other cultures, ideas, and thinking.

Final Thought

Lifelong learning is not just about professional success; it is about personal enrichment, adaptability, and a fulfilling life. Whether through structured education, real-world experiences, or everyday observations, the pursuit of knowledge shapes a better future. The world belongs to those who never stop learning.

Chapter 16: Creating an Inclusive Workplace

In today's rapidly changing professional world, the key to success is not innovation, or revenue, or individual genius. It is the culture we establish in our organizations. One of the most distinctive characteristics of a healthy culture is inclusivity. An inclusive work environment is not just a diversity checkbox or a politically correct phrase. It is a vibrant community where everyone, irrespective of background, ability, or opinion, feels valued, heard, and empowered.

An inclusive workplace doesn't just serve members from underrepresented groups; it serves the entire organization. When individuals feel free to be themselves, innovation flourishes. When perspectives are shared, problem-solving improves. And when leaders pledge equity, loyalty and trust ensue.

But inclusivity doesn't occur by accident. It takes intention, awareness, and ongoing learning. It takes empathetic leaders, open-minded teams, and systems that encourage fairness. One of the drivers of an inclusive workplace is the desire to get past personal failures and take others along the way. In these workplaces, individuals don't compete by tearing others down but grow by lifting others up.

In this chapter, we are going to discuss the importance of inclusion using Muntazir's life as an example. This young man learns that failure can occur at the individual level but results in collective power. In his journey of collapse and resurgence, we realize how incorporation is about accepting failure, learning from failures, and making room for every voice to have value. When the workplace is diverse, even a fallen person can get up, but not alone, with the help and guidance of a community that has faith in them.

Story

In a small town, there was a young man called Muntazir. He was famous near and far because of his brilliant mind and uncompromising determination. Right from childhood, he was a student and sports champion, and it was said about him that he was born for greatness. His parents beamed with pride, his teachers were full of praises, and his friends looked up to him.

But when Muntazir reached adulthood, the wind changed. Praise became pressure, and confidence gradually became overconfidence. Convinced that his natural ability would be enough to see him through, Muntazir began to slack off. He abandoned the disciplines that had made him sparkle. He avoided practice, put off homework, and wasted countless hours binge-watching films and scrolling through his phone.

His parents tried to guide him gently, reminding him that success wasn't permanent, and failure wasn't final. But Muntazir, lost in the illusion of past achievements, brushed off their concerns. "I know what I'm doing," he'd say, flashing his signature grin.

Then came the final exam results.

To his dismay and surprise, Muntazir had flunked two subjects. For the first time in his life, the top boy who was always at the top was at the bottom. His once-back-patting teachers now shook their heads in despair. His friends started avoiding him. The silence from home was more painful than any act of chastisement ever could have been.

Distraught, Muntazir shut himself up in his room. He went over every step, wondering what went wrong. Days went by. Shame enveloped his heart, and self-doubt entered his head.

One evening, as the twilight colored the sky in shades of orange and blue, his grandfather tapped at the door gently and entered. He was a man of few words but of boundless wisdom. He spoke little, and the silence settled between them.

Then, in his soft voice, he asked, "Do you know how a phoenix is born again?"

Muntazir, perplexed and somewhat annoyed, shook his head.

"When the phoenix ages, it constructs a nest and ignites itself. It burns to ash. Yet from those very ashes, it is reborn — stronger, wiser, and more beautiful. Life is similar. At times, we have to burn in the flames of our errors to rise once again."

"But I failed, Grandpa. I'm not who I used to be. Everything is lost," Muntazir whispered.

Grandpa nodded thoughtfully. "Let me tell you a story."

He began the tale of a mighty king named Zafar, once known for his courage and intelligence. Under his rule, the kingdom prospered. But success blinded him. He stopped preparing his army, ignored his ministers, and believed nothing could ever go wrong.

There came a day when an enemy kingdom invaded. The once great army was not ready. The kingdom was lost, and Zafar ran into the wilderness, defeated and shamed. He lived in the mountains, far from human society, fighting guilt and loneliness.

One day, he observed an ant trying to carry a grain of rice up a rock. The ant slipped, fell, and kept on trying again and again. It never gave up. On its twelfth try, it made it.

He watched and he understood. If an ant never gives up, why should a king? He rebuilt his life with deliberate slowness and humility. Years later, he came back, stronger and wiser. He regained his kingdom, but this time, he ruled with humility, discipline, and love.

Muntazir listened, his eyes wide.

"Failure is a lesson," his grandfather had told him. "An opportunity to add new ideas, individuals, and fields of study to your world. The world does not reject the ones who stumble. It waits to discover who will get up."

For the first time in days, Muntazir felt something change within him.

"What do I do next, Grandpa?"

"Begin by admitting your failure. Then plan. Little steps. Every day efforts. And always, never walk alone. Get other people involved. Let your parents guide you, your friends accompany you, and your teachers be with you. Build your strength not alone, but together."

Muntazir started anew. He removed his social media applications, rearranged his day, and established a study habit. He asked teachers for additional support and started assisting fellow students who struggled with specific subjects.

In supporting others, he saw himself improve. In being helped, he gained new power. Gradually but steadily, he improved.

When the subsequent results were out, Muntazir did not merely pass. He led the class.

His narrative was a legend in the town, not because he never faltered, but because he learned how to rise up and share his success with others.

Actionable Insights

Creating an inclusive workplace starts with an attitude — the idea that every person, regardless of their history or previous record, has something to offer. Muntazir's story illustrates failure isn't an ending but commonly a starting point of deeper insights and understanding. Within professional spheres, this episode recurs daily: one of a group performs worse, an individual hitches along in a fresh area, or one worker crashes. The point is not so much that we fall as whether or how well we bounce back.

Here are some real-time actions toward cultivating a warm environment where each employee can spring up again.

1. Normalize Failure: Establish a culture in which errors are viewed as chances for growth instead of excuses for exclusion. Open communication about failures and setbacks is encouraged. When leaders acknowledge their failures, it establishes a precedent for honesty and development.

2. Give Access to Support: As Muntazir sought assistance, workers need access to coaches, mental health services, and skill development resources. Providing peer mentorship opportunities and open discussion spaces can make a big difference.

3. Reward Effort, Not Outcome Alone: Commend steady effort even if outcomes are not optimum. If work is valued by people, it will motivate them to remain productive and develop steadily over time.

4. Teach Collaboration: Indulge in group assignments, team learning events, and multidisciplinary work. Diversity does best when distinct viewpoints are welcomed as much as sought after.

5. Create Feedback Loops: Provide regular, constructive feedback on behavior and ways to improve. Feedback should

build up, not break down. Make it specific, considerate, and actionable.

6. Hire and Promote Diversely: Hire and promote for potential and dedication, rather than history. Look for grit, resilience, and flexibility — qualities that typically surface after a fall.

An inclusive workplace not only provides second chances but a culture where people rise from the ashes is respected and nurtured. Like Muntazir, all deserve a place where they can discover their potential and make a positive contribution to a shared future. Inclusion, after all, is not an act of charity. It's a recipe for long-term success.

Recurs daily: one of a group performs worse, an individual hitches along in a fresh area, or one worker crashes. The point is not so much that we fall as whether or how well we bounce back.

Here are some real-time actions toward cultivating a warm environment where each employee can spring up again:

1. Normalize Failure: Establish a culture in which errors are viewed as chances for growth instead of excuses for exclusion. Open communication about failures and setbacks is

encouraged. When leaders acknowledge their failures, it establishes a precedent for honesty and development.

2. Give Access to Support: As Muntazir sought assistance, workers need access to coaches, mental health services, and skill development resources. Providing peer mentorship opportunities and open discussion spaces can make a big difference.

3. Reward Effort, Not Outcome Alone: Commend steady effort even if outcomes are not optimum. If work is valued by people, it will motivate them to remain productive and develop steadily over time.

4. Teach Collaboration: Indulge in group assignments, team learning events, and multidisciplinary work. Diversity does best when distinct viewpoints are welcomed as much as sought after.

5. Create Feedback Loops: Provide regular, constructive feedback on behavior and ways to improve. Feedback should build up, not break down. Make it specific, considerate, and actionable.

6. Hire and Promote Diversely: Hire and promote for potential and dedication, rather than history. Look for grit,

resilience, and flexibility — qualities that typically surface after a fall.

An inclusive workplace not only provides second chances but a culture where people rise from the ashes is respected and nurtured. Like Muntazir, all deserve a place where they can discover their potential and make a positive contribution to a shared future. Inclusion, after all, is not an act of charity. It's a recipe for long-term success.

Chapter 17: Going the Extra Mile

There's that special something about going the extra mile. It's that certain spark that takes the ordinary to the extraordinary. It's not necessarily about genius or talent, but about persistence, determination, and the inclination to do more than is required. In whatever field of endeavor—whether student, artist, entrepreneur, scientist—the ones who stand out above the rest are the ones who go beyond expectations.

We exist in a world that too often celebrates the mediocre. You do what you're told, you listen, you check the boxes. That's sufficient. Is it though? The reality is, greatness doesn't begin with doing the minimum. It begins with getting up when you don't want to, with trying again after you've failed, and with pushing your limits when convenience calls on you to settle.

Doing the extra mile is not only a career choice; it's a lifestyle. It's what makes a hobby a job, an idea a movement, and an individual a legend. It's the doing when all your body and mind are screaming at you to quit.

This chapter delves into this transformational thinking through one of the greatest tales of contemporary human grit—the life of Stephen Hawking. In spite of every possible hindrance, he emerged as a science icon in the world. Not because he was the genius of the class, but because when life attempted to take him down, he pushed harder.

His is a beacon of inspiration for what occurs when you don't give up. When you don't simply walk the path—but take that extra mile.

Story

Stephen Hawking was not born a genius. Indeed, when he was younger, nothing about him shouted genius. He struggled to learn how to read and was by no means at the top of his class. School reports frequently termed him lazy, unmotivated, and unfocused. Yet his teachers did see something different. A weird glint in his eye. A spark. An insistent curiosity that couldn't be harnessed by the school course.

Education meant a great deal to his family. His father and mother both came from Oxford University, and evenings at home meant dinner parties featuring passionate debate over science, literature, and philosophy. Stephen? He tinkered with whatever object was around him—breaking things down to pieces, fabricating gadgets, and concocting bizarre systems of mechanics. He was affectionately known at school as "Einstein," but not due to his grade-point average. Rather, his odd perspective about life earned him this nickname.

Stephen arrived at Oxford University at age seventeen, where he studied physics and chemistry. You'd expect this to be where his genius kicked in. But no—Stephen, by his own account, was fantastically lazy while in school. He'd work as little as less than an hour a day at times. "I'm not proud of it," he admitted once. "But it's the truth. I just didn't think that anything was worth the effort." It wasn't arrogance. It was lack of interest.

But that changed.

He went to Cambridge after Oxford to study for a PhD in cosmology. It was there, just as his academic journey was starting to make sense, that life dealt him a crushing blow. He began to notice strange things—he was more clumsy than normal, his words started to slur, and he would stumble and fall for no reason. At first, he dismissed it. But things worsened. Tests were conducted. Hospital visits followed. Then came the diagnosis that shattered his world.

At age 21, Stephen Hawking was told he had ALS—amyotrophic lateral sclerosis—a motor neuron disease that is very rare. Doctors predicted he would only live two years. His body would gradually turn off. He would lose control of walking, speaking, eating, breathing. In a lot of ways, it was a death sentence given to someone who was just starting to get life figured out.

Anyone else would have crumpled under that news. And Stephen did—at first. He turned inward, depressed. He quit working, wondering what the use of it was. But then something shifted. He met Jane Wilde, a life-filled and empathetic literature student. Love entered his life, and with it came meaning. With Jane by his side, Stephen decided that if life was going to be brief, it would at least be meaningful.

And so, he started to battle on—not against the illness, but against the temptation to surrender.

He threw himself into his work. He decided to do the extra step, even when the extra step seemed impossible. Day by day, while his body failed him, his mind opened up. With fingers that could barely move, he scribbled down equations. With speech that was barely possible, he lectured in revolutionary ways. When he was no longer able to speak, he relied on a speech synthesizer—and adopted that computer-generated voice as his own trademark sound.

The man who used to work less than an hour a day now worked around the clock—his mind became his sanctuary, and then his tool.

Stephen's research on black holes and the creation of the universe did not only bring him academic renown; it revolutionized the field of physics forever. His book A Brief History of Time was sold over 10 million copies, and it became a phenomenon in scientific and popular culture.

But it wasn't his scientific contributions alone that touched millions of people—it was his spirit. His refusal to be defeated by disease. His humor, his charm, his clarity in the midst of chaos. Even after being informed he had just two years to live, he survived more than 55. He raised a family, traveled the globe, worked with artists and musicians, guest-starred on The Simpsons and Star Trek, and even wheeled himself onto the set of The Big Bang Theory.

He never complained of his illness when questioned. "It is a waste of time to be angry about my disability," he once ventured. "One has to get on with life, and I haven't done badly."

Stephen Hawking's life teaches us that genius is never sufficient. Life will and does test you—roughly, unexpectedly, and unjustly. What you do once the test starts is what counts. Do you quit? Or do you push beyond?

He was wheelchair-bound, but his mind explored galaxies.

Ultimately, his message to humanity was simple, strong, indelible:

"Be curious. No matter how hard things seem, there is always something you can do and get better at. It's important that you don't just quit. Be brave, be determined, beat the odds. It is possible. As long as there is life, there is hope."

Actionable Insights: Going the Extra Mile in Your Own Life

1. Choose Progress Over Perfection

Stephen Hawking didn't wait until he was in the ideal shape, ideal mood, or ideal environment to begin working. He worked in spite of everything. Doing the extra mile is doing small, steady steps even when everything isn't ideal. Progress is more important than polish.

Ask yourself: What's one thing I can do today to make progress? It doesn't have to be big—it just has to be done.

2. Redefine Limitations

Most individuals let their limitations—real or perceived—hold them back. But limitations are usually beginnings in disguise. Hawking's physical condition might have prevented him from even attempting it. Instead, he utilized his mind, his curiosity, and subsequently, technology to fill in every gap.

Begin by changing your internal conversation. Rather than "I can't," say "How can I?" Your mind is programmed to discover solutions—but only if you think solutions are possible to discover.

3. Create Meaningful Habits

When all else is up in the air, routines anchor us. Hawking had a rigorous schedule and a definite sense of direction. Building a routine around your objectives—whether it's studying, exercising, or writing—assists in translating ambition into action. The extra mile starts with daily miles that might be dull but build results over time.

4. Find Your Why

Stephen Hawking's 'why' only made sense once he was about to die. You don't need to get a death sentence, however, to identify your own. Take some time getting to know what compels you. People, passion, and purpose are all mighty motivators. After identifying your 'why', even the most challenging miles will seem to be worthwhile.

5. Refuse to Be Defined by Your Circumstances

Life might deal you with injustice. You might be ignored, underestimated, or discouraged. But what you do in those times is what makes you who you are. Hawking was never merely his diagnosis. He was his work, his sense of humor, his determination.

You too are not your failures, your past, or your fears. You are your determination. Be the person who doesn't stop at the red light, but asks, "Can I build a bridge instead?"

6. Commit Publicly. Act Privately.

Inform someone of your ambitions. But most importantly, arrive when nobody is looking. Extra effort is over glorified. It's in the unglamorous late nights, the subtle adjustments, the readiness to redo, retry, and relearn.

When the tough gets going, the extra mile starts. And though it's perhaps the loneliest part of the road, it's also where miracles are made.

So, don't stop when it's hard. That's exactly when it matters most.

Go on. Walk that extra mile. You never know how far it might take you.

Chapter 18: Habits

Good and bad habits determine the beat of our lives. They are the unseen structure behind our everyday decisions, the unobtrusive leaders of our energy, time, and emotional capital. Our habits influence not only what we do but also how we think and feel, whether it is how we begin the day, how we engage with others, or how we handle stress.

But what truly sets successful people apart from the rest is the habits they form along the way, not their skill or intelligence. Small, steady habits start to form the foundation for discipline, toughness, and optimism. With distractions now manifesting in the form of constant scrolling and the pressure to respond immediately, the practice of keeping your eyes on what matters is more important than ever before.

This chapter is a friendly reminder about a simple reality: what you put your focus on expands. If you put attention into gossip, bad stuff, and static around you, it blows up and steals your energy. But if you anchor your intention into your aims, your sense of peace, and your principles, then they bloom instead.

The story that follows—a timeless parable from the world of monks—doesn't preach complex theories. Instead, it demonstrates a powerful message using an everyday metaphor: a spoonful of water. Through this tale, we're invited to examine how much of our own energy is spilt by paying attention to distractions that do not serve us. It's not just about ignoring negativity; it's about building the habit of attention management.

So while you're reading, ask yourself—what are the spoonfuls of water in your life that you have to carry with care and intention? And what can you begin tuning out today, so you can tune into the life you're supposed to live?

The Story

In a peaceful hill-top monastery covered with tall cedar trees and resonating chants of monks, a young disciple by the name of Tenzin went to meet his master early one morning. His eyes were not sleepy, but weighed down with the frustration that had gathered within him over the weeks.

"Master," he replied, his voice shaking with a combination of rage and powerlessness, "I cannot remain here anymore. I must go. Let me go to another monastery—somewhere peaceful, somewhere... better."

The master, a silver-haired old man with wisdom strands in his beard and the peace of the mountains in his eyes, raised his head to look at Tenzin. "Why, my child? What is it that bothers you here?"

Tenzin did not hesitate. "This is a toxic environment. Some monks spend all day gossiping behind one another's backs. Others are involved in temple politics, constantly seeking to acquire power or influence. And then there are those who never utter anything nice—only criticism, complaints, and negativity. I cannot devote myself to my spiritual path under such circumstances.

The master nodded ponderously and then slowly got up from his chair. "Very well," he said, "I'll let you go. But before that, will you do me a favor?"

"Anything, master. Certainly.

He was given a spoon by the elderly monk. He said, "I want you to walk around the monastery grounds—every path, every hall, every corner—and come back to me without spilling a single drop from this spoon." He had taken a spoonful of water from the brass bowl on the altar.

Tenzin arched an eyebrow, curious but bewildered. "That's it?"

"That's it."

With utmost care, Tenzin departed. Eyes intently focused on the shaking water in the spoon, he moved slowly, carefully, his entire self attuned to the motion of the water. He walked around the prayer hall, crept along the stone path in the garden, worked his way through the dining quarters, and glided past every single monk without even looking at them. Hours went by. His arms began to ache, his legs weary, but he stood firm, resolute.

At last, he came back to the master, holding up the spoon victoriously.

"Here, master. Not a single drop spilled."

A pleased smile tingled on the lips of the old monk. "Good work. Now, before you go, ask me this—on your walk, did you hear any monks gossiping?"

"No," replied Tenzin, taken aback.

"Did you see anyone indulging in politics or someone condemning others?"

"No," he confessed, "I was concentrating too hard on not spilling the water.

The master's smile grew. "Just like that, my son. You were so intent on your work that all the commotion around you became as silent as a still room. The same with your life. You won't even be aware of the distractions and negativity surrounding you if you focus on your goals, your beliefs, and your personal development. However, you will lose your time, energy, and peace the moment your thoughts stray to what other people are saying or doing.

Tenzin stayed there, the lesson sinking deep into his heart like a gentle snowfall. "So it's not the monastery that's toxic," he breathed, "it's what I choose to focus on."

The master nodded. "You can go to the quietest monastery in the world, but even there, you'll find flaws. Not because the people are flawed—but because our mind will always look for what it chooses to see. Choose to see with focus. Choose to see with kindness."

The young monk stared at the spoon in his hand as if he had never seen one before. A tool, a teacher, a mirror. And in that instant, he realized something that most of us spend our entire lives searching for: peace is not at a perfect destination—it is at a concentrated mind.

After that day, Tenzin remained at the monastery. He still overheard the occasional rumor, still encountered the monks who played politics, still walked among critics. But he walked past them as he did that day with the spoonful of water—in quiet, unshakeable concentration.

And bit by bit, as his inner landscape transformed, so did the world outside.

Actionable Insights

The story of the student monk is not a fable—it's a lesson in creating strong habits that can change how we live, work, and react to the world. Here are a few takeaways to integrate into your daily life:

1. Focus is a habit

As with the student monk who concentrated on the spoonful of water, so too can we condition our minds to concentrate on what's really important. Start every morning by setting your number one to three priorities—activities that connect to your ultimate purpose. Hold them as your guide. The more you become deliberate in focusing, the easier it gets to make it second nature.

2. You can't control others, only yourself

There will always be criticism, unproductive gossip, or negativity surrounding you—on social media, in your own family, or at work. Rather than wanting the world to change, practice the habit of turning your attention inward. Ask yourself, How can I react to this with grace and clarity rather than an emotional response?

3. Mindfulness over multitasking

Most of us boast about multitasking, but really we're watering down our attention. The monk who focused on the spoon instead of playing detective with gossip demonstrates how mindfulness practice helps one achieve concentration. Try performing activities as solo operations, such as consuming lunch while responding to emails during your downtime and engaging with your friends.

4. Positivity is a choice

When you're faced with negativity, you have a choice—either to soak it up or to be above it. Reply with positivity. Don't reflect someone else's bitterness; rather, model the behavior you desire. Someday, that energy becomes a habit, and that habit becomes your identity.

5. Refocus daily

Each day is a chance to reboot back to your larger picture. At bedtime, take five minutes to reflect: Did I invest more time centered on my development, or was I drawn in by distractions? The first step towards changing a habit is awareness.

In a loud world, people who get good at the focus and positivity elevate above—it isn't that their world gets quieter, it's that their minds are more resilient.

Chapter 19: Living Humility and Gratitude

Success intoxicates. It comes with applause, spotlight, opportunity—and occasionally, pride. The world honors success quickly, yet tends to forget to remind us of the two things that ground authentic greatness: thankfulness and humility. These aren't feel-good feelings or lofty virtues reserved for the ages—they are habits of a lifetime, hammered out in quiet, that save us from being victims of our success.

Thank you represents only one aspect of gratitude, while it features a broader perspective as a whole. This mental outlook enables people to direct their attention from missing elements to existing aspects. When practised daily, gratitude both transforms your perspective into one of gratitude and grants you generosity while helping you see that your progress resulted from your hard work and also the support and kindness of others. Repeated daily practice of gratitude produces a reflection that demonstrates the interlinked nature of your progression.

Humility, by contrast, is not about putting yourself down. It's having the fortitude to acknowledge complimenting words without letting it fill your ego balloon. Humility shows you your own size within the big picture. It builds trust, solicits candid input, and attracts others to you—not for what you've achieved, but because of the manner in which you carry it all.".

In a world that constantly pushes you to stand out, humility keeps you on the ground. In a world that does not teach cooperation but competition, gratitude makes you connect.

To live with both is to journey through life with equilibrium—eyes raised in aspiration, but feet rooted in the ground of vision.

This chapter isn't just a moral reminder—it's a practical guide. Through a powerful story and evidence-backed habits, we'll exp re how to live gratitude and humility as daily practices, and ow they quietly compound into extraordinary influence and inner peace.

The Emperor and the Monk: A Tale from the Kingdom of Magadha

A young prince named Ajatashatru spent his days in the ancient Magadha kingdom, which contained ferocious warriors together with fertile lands. Ajatashatru dedicated all his education to expertise in war and received his royal training from top scholars while living in luxury during his youth to achieve one goal: becoming Magadha's most excellent king that surpassing his father, King Bimbisara.

After his father contracted an illness, Ajatashatru became king. During his first years as ruler, he achieved multiple victories through expanding his realm while building magnificent accomplishments and sustaining prosperous markets. His life transformed into legend during his own time period, and he received glory through songs as well as temple wall inscriptions.

Power started to change him in a negative way because it has a known tendency to distort those who obtain it. Due to his impatience, he adopted an arrogant attitude toward his ministers alongside contemptuous behaviour. To Ajatashatru, all spiritual leaders were worthy of mockery since he believed humility served only weak people. The royal crown he held remained fixed deep inside his inner soul instead of being visibly worn upon his head.

A royal procession encountered an abrupt storm when it happened one day. The dark storm clouds turned absolutely black as thunder released mighty noises similar to nationalist battle cries. At the edge of the forest, a modest monastery was located where the emperor's retinue stopped to seek refuge. Ajatashatru showed his displeasure by ordering guards to retrieve the monk who led the monastery for his entertainment.

An elderly monk with a thin figure approached, carrying a gentle expression on his bare feet. With deep respect, he welcomed the king, presuming his position.

Ajatashatru scoffed. "You reside in this hut and proclaim yourself wise? Inform me, old man, what knowledge do you possess of the world I govern?"

The monk merely replied, "Only what the winds carry, Your Highness. But if it pleases you, may I present you with a bowl of rice prepared by our youngest disciple?

The emperor grinned but consented. As the monk departed, Ajatashatru ridiculed, "Let's see if these monks can cook at least!"

The rice was set before him in a coarse clay bowl—steaming, pungent, and unpretentious. Ajatashatru's scowl softened when he tasted. It was the plainest thing he had had to eat for years—and it was somehow soothing. He went on eating till the bowl was clean.

"Who prepared this?" he demanded.

The monk smiled. "A boy who was once abandoned by his parents and adopted by us. He's never uttered a word, but he bows with thanks every time someone takes his food."

Something moved in the emperor. He glanced around the hut—there were no golden walls, no large paintings, only scrolls, scriptures, and quiet. The monk went on:

"Majesty, kings establish empires. But empires fall. What remains is not what you dominate, but how you are remembered."

Ajatashatru, half smiling, replied, "And how do I get remembered well?"

The monk replied, "By being thankful for what you have, and modest about what you've done. Thankfulness reminds you that no throne is ascended alone. And modesty reminds you that even emperors bleed red."

The emperor departed that day, silent and reflective.

Years went by. With Ajatashatru as king, Magadha prospered—but something was different. He started to visit orphanages unnoticed, giving alms to the poor, and taking counsel from sages before he made decisions. He treated his slaves with unusual compassion, and when his sculptors came to him and said that they didn't know how to cut his figure in stone, he replied, "With one hand raised in benediction—and the other at my chest, where humility dwells."

Late in his years, one day a foreign traveller stopped him and said, "What was the greatest thing you ever learned when you were king?"

Ajatashatru answered, "That I am merely a man in borrowed crown. Gratitude reminded me to thank the past. Humility instructed me to serve the future."

And many years after his passing, that monk's hut stood, not for its wealth, but for the emperor who knelt there.

Actionable Insights

1. Practice Gratitude as a Daily Habit
Gratitude is not a warm, fuzzy sensation—it's a skill. You can build it daily with small, consistent habits:

- Keep a gratitude journal: Each morning or evening, list 3 things you appreciate. They don't have to be big—enjoy clean water, a nice word, or a stress-free commute.

- Voice appreciation: Express thanks to the people who help your work get done—your colleagues, your significant other, the individual who brings you tea. Don't leave it implicit—say it out loud.

- Reframe complaints: Replace phrases like "I have to do this" with phrases like "I get to do this." A change in language changes a perspective.

- Gratitude triggers: Link gratitude to habits that already exist. For example, each time you wash your hands, think to thank your body for its function.

Gratitude lifts your mood, strengthens your relationships, and even improves your sleep and physical health.

2. Practice Humility in Success

Humility isn't thinking less of yourself—it's thinking of yourself less. It's staying teachable, even when you're the expert. Here's how:

- Credit others often: When praised, deflect the spotlight to your team. Success is rarely a solo act.

- Listen more, talk less: Answer fewer questions than you ask. Others will not only respect you but also look up to you, not because of your dominance but because of your curiosity.

- Know when you don't know: "I don't know" is a sign of strength. It invites cooperation and learning.

- Make success a platform for service: Whether through mentoring someone, giving anonymously, or lifting others up, use your success to have a ripple effect.

- Have symbols of humility nearby: A childhood picture, a note written by a mentor, or even a clay bowl can serve as a reminder of where you began.

3. Why It Matters
Gratitude makes you likeable. Humility makes you trustworthy. Together, they make you magnetic.

Whether you're a CEO, a student, or a freelancer, your legacy won't just be your success. It will be how you treated people when you had the power not to.

Success glows brightest when it's illuminated from the inside.

Chapter 20: Leaving a Legacy

Our existence revolves around seeking out specific achievements, which include degree achievements and promotions, along with monetary success and public recognition. Nonetheless, they serve as visible outcomes which can be measured as well as validated by social acceptance. After the noise fades, we ask ourselves a different question, which materialises in the content of our lives rather than counting achievements. People tend to reflect on their lives by asking themselves what they left unsaid.

A lasting legacy is not established through building inscriptions with your name or obtaining widespread internet recognition. Your succession of choices alongside your core values and personal activities creates this effect. Life leaves an impact through people's emotions rather than newspapers' historical records. Your legacy produces better choices and complete life fulfilment and daring dreams, which emerge through the seeds you plant today.

Success does not equal significance in its essence. The experience of success usually persists only during the current times and fades as soon as these moments end. Significance echoes beyond your time. Think about it: medals rust, careers end, even fortunes can vanish. But the way you mentored someone, the values you passed to your children, the kindness you showed to strangers—that endures.

Leaving a legacy isn't a retirement goal. It's a daily practice. It begins when you stop asking, "What can I get?" and start asking, "What can I give?" It deepens when you understand that influence doesn't require fame—it requires intention.

This chapter is an invitation to reflect on how you want to be remembered—not by many, but by the few who truly matter. Through a story from the past and actionable steps, you'll discover how legacy isn't about building monuments—it's about building meaning.

The Story: The Cobbler of Varanasi

In the crowded alleys of old Varanasi, near the ghats where the Ganga whispers ancient secrets, lived an old cobbler named Bhairav. His shop wasn't really a shop—it was a corner under a neem tree with a wooden plank, a few tools, and a lamp that burned long into the night.

Bhairav was not wealthy, not widely known, and never went to school. But he was a legend in that part of the city. Not because he fixed sandals better than anyone else—though he did—but because of how he lived.

He greeted every customer, rich or poor, with folded hands and a soft "Ram Ram." He never charged the poor and never overcharged the rich. He fed stray dogs every evening before he ate himself. If a child came with a torn slipper, he'd offer a quick fix and a sweet, saying, "Walk strong, little one."

Most people never knew where he came from. Some whispered he was once a soldier who gave up violence. Others said he was a widower who chose to serve rather than mourn. But Bhairav never talked about his past. He only smiled, worked, and served.

One monsoon, a major flood hit Varanasi. Temples were submerged, homes destroyed, and disease followed. Government relief was delayed. But Bhairav showed up every day at the ghat. He turned his little spot into a help center. He stitched shoes for free for people who lost theirs in the flood. He gave away his savings to buy water filters. He taught children to chant simple prayers to calm their panic. Local shopkeepers began pooling resources around him. His spot became the first organized relief hub before the government aid even arrived.

A journalist passing through town wrote a small piece about him: "The cobbler who led a city with his hands and heart."

Years later, Bhairav passed away quietly in his sleep. He had no family, no heir, no property. But his funeral procession drew thousands. People carried garlands, not banners. They didn't chant slogans—they sang bhajans. Children placed flowers by his tree. The mayor of Varanasi attended, uninvited, and wept.

Years turned into decades. The neem tree still stands. And every year, on the day of his passing, locals gather to serve food, clean sandals, and tell stories of Bhairav to the younger generation.

There is no statue of him. But every child in that part of Varanasi knows his name.

A young man who once had torn shoes is now a lawyer. He funds education for cobbler families.

A woman whose brother died in the floods runs a non-profit in Bhairav's name.

His impact outlived him. Not because he chased greatness—but because he chose goodness.

Legacy, as Bhairav proved, isn't what you leave in your will. It's what you leave in people's lives.

Actionable Insights

1. Reflect on What You Want to Be Remembered For
Legacy starts with clarity. Ask yourself:

- What values do I want people to associate with me? Is it kindness, courage, generosity, creativity?
- Who do I want to impact most—my family, my community, my profession, or a cause?
- What stories do I want people to tell about me when I'm gone?

Write a "legacy statement"—a short paragraph that defines the essence of your desired impact. Revisit it annually. Let it guide your decisions, especially the tough ones.

2. Start Living That Legacy Today
Legacy is not built in one grand gesture. It's formed in daily habits:

- Mentor someone younger: Pass on what you've learned. Knowledge is the most underrated inheritance.

- Give without expecting recognition: Anonymous impact often lasts longer than public applause.

- Capture your stories and lessons: Write a journal, record videos, or create a blog—not to go viral, but to be passed on.

- Uphold values, especially when inconvenient: That's when they leave a lasting impression.

Remember, small consistent acts shape how you're remembered far more than one-time grand achievements.

3. Create Structures That Outlive You

While legacy is often intangible, you can also institutionalize your values:

- Start a scholarship or support fund in your name or someone you admire.

- Plant trees, support a library, or back a community center—things that keep giving after you're gone.

- Document family stories and wisdom—create a digital archive, photo books, or audio clips.

- If you run a business, define a values charter. Create traditions that last even without you.

4. Understand That Legacy Is a Process, Not a Product
You don't have to be perfect to leave a legacy. In fact, the most powerful legacies often come from those who grew through failures, admitted mistakes, and still chose to give back.

Legacy is a slow burn. It's a letter written in invisible ink—seen clearly only after you're gone.

But when lived intentionally, it becomes your echo. Quiet. Powerful. And everlasting.

Verses Kindler Publication

Verses Kindler Publication

Reach us through our website -
https://www.verseskindlerpublication.com/
For more information visit our Instagram or Facebook page.